Remembering

Remembering

Favorite Memories of Walt Disney

By

AMY BOOTHE GREEN & HOWARD E. GREEN

Foreword by

RAY BRADBURY

HYPERION

NEW YORK

All photos © by Disney Enterprises, Inc., except for page ii, courtesy of Diane Disney
Miller; pages 20-21, courtesy of Bob Moore; page 48, courtesy of Harrison Ellenshaw;
page 64, courtesy of Floyd Norman; page 80, courtesy of Lucille Martin; page 132,
courtesy of Richard Fleischer; and page 148, courtesy of Ward Kimball.

Library of Congress Cataloging-in-Publication Data

Green, Amy Boothe.
        Remembering Walt : favorite memories of Walt Disney / by Amy
Boothe Green & Howard E. Green ; foreword by Ray Bradbury.--1st ed.
              p.   cm.
        ISBN 0-7868-6348-X
        1. Disney, Walt, 1901-1966.   2. Animators--United States--
Biography.   I. Green, Howard E.   II. Title.
NC1766.U52D5423   1999
791.43'092--dc21
[B]   99-10491
                              CIP

First Edition
10 9 8 7 6 5 4 3 2 1

Contents

FOREWORD

BY RAY BRADBURY

WALT DISNEY was more important than all the politicians we've ever had. They pretended optimism. He *was* optimism. He has done more to change the world for the good than almost any politician who ever lived.

I'm talking about the influences of mind and imagination on people. I'm talking about culture and individuals' imaginations, which change that culture.

I first met Walt Disney at Saks Fifth Avenue. I saw this man coming across the floor with a huge armload of Christmas gifts and his head tucked over the top. I looked at that face and said, "Oh my God, it's my hero," because I fell in love with *Steamboat Willie* and *The Skeleton Dance* when I was eight years old. I always wanted to work for Disney and Walt, so I ran up to him and said, "Mr. Disney…"

"Yes?" he replied.

"My name's Ray Bradbury."

"I know your books," he said.

"Thank God!" I exclaimed.

"Why?"

"Because sometime soon I'd like to take you to lunch," I said.

And then Walt said the most wonderful thing…*"Tomorrow!"* Isn't that beautiful?! When's the last time you ever had someone say "tomorrow"? They say, "next week" or "next month."

So I went to lunch with him the next day. I couldn't believe it. And we sat in his office at a card table, ate soup and salad and sandwiches and babbled like a couple of kids. I raved about how I used to go to the county museum, when I was fourteen years old, to stare at *Steamboat Willie, Flowers and Trees,* and *The Skeleton Dance* cels. Every Sunday I stared at the same damned cels as if I couldn't drink in enough! God, I wanted to *own* some of those! So here I was at last meeting Walt and talking with him!

We discussed rapid transit because I had formed a group called PRIME: Promote Rapid Transit Improve Metropolitan Environment. Rapid transit was dying in Los Angeles. They'd eliminated all the street cars—stupid. I told Walt about my group and how I was trying to improve Los Angeles, which was hopeless. I said, "Walt, I wish you would run for mayor."

"Ray," he said, "why should I be mayor when I'm already king!"

I visited Disneyland for the first time with my actor friend Charles

Laughton. We flew over London and stared down at Big Ben. When we got aboard the jungle ride, Charles Laughton became Captain Bligh, barking orders, keelhauling pirates. When I described this to Walt, he was delighted.

Later, I wrote a whole series of articles about future cities and defended Disneyland against the New York intellectuals. Remembering this, Walt said, "Ray, you've done so much for us. What can *we* do for *you?*

"Walt," I said, "open the vaults!"

So he picked up the phone, called across the street and said, "Open the vaults, I'm sending Ray over. He can have *anything* he wants." I went over to the animation vaults and carried out an armload of cels from *Snow White, Sleeping Beauty, Alice in Wonderland.* I felt guilty, but elated. I couldn't stop stacking. The kid who went to the museum when he was fourteen and saw the *The Skeleton Dance* cels and wanted them…now, *had* them.

The day of Walt's memorial service, I took my four daughters to Disneyland. We'd planned to go long before Walt's death. When we got home late that night, my wife Maggie said, "CBS Radio called this afternoon and wanted to interview you about Walt. I said you were at Disneyland with the kids." At this, I burst into tears. I said, "My God, what a tribute! A *real* tribute to a wonderful man."

Today, when I lecture, people ask me, "Are you a pessimist?"

"No," I say. "That's a lie."

"Are you an optimist?"

"No. That's a lie."

"Well, what the hell are you?" they ask.

"I'm an optimal behaviorist, like Disney," I reply. With a grand sense of fun and passion, you're going to create something fine. Not always, but Walt was a bursting fountain, always running at full speed. *That* makes for optimal behavior. Behaving at the peak of genetic madness.

Walt left the world a thousand times better than when he arrived. He personified Schweitzer's quote: "Do something good. Someone may imitate it."

$\mathcal{I}$NTRODUCTION

Once upon a time not so very long ago, in a fanciful realm called Southern California, there lived a miraculous man named Walt Disney who ruled over a vast magical kingdom of his own making. His subjects were loyal and his fans were many. He was a dreamer, a doer, and a master of imagination.

While a chorus of nay-sayers bellowed, "Can't Do," this man exemplified "Can Do" because in his mind, no idea was too small and no vision was too tall to pursue. He dedicated his life to fun, fantasy, and the pursuit of happiness and as the pied piper of possibility, like minds followed his call, and together they transformed an entire world.

TRY TO IMAGINE a world without Walt Disney. Imagine a world without his magic, whimsy, and optimism. During his sixty-five-year life, Walt Disney changed many things. He transformed the face of the entertainment industry, animation, and education. He was a giant, a legend about whom more has been written than any other entertainment personality of this century, with the exception of Charlie Chaplin, who, coincidentally, was one of Walt's heroes and main sources of inspiration.

Walt Disney changed the lives of those who knew him—and those who didn't know him. Those of us who didn't know Walt personally, certainly felt as *if* we knew him. We remember *Uncle Walt* for his generous gifts to us ranging from the animated fairy tales he spun and the Magic Kingdom he built in a California orange grove, to his Sunday night visits into our living rooms. He brought "color" into our worlds and opened our minds to the thrill of creating just about anything we could possibly imagine.

Walt Disney was our bridge from fantasy to reality, challenging our perceptions of both. Is reality really reality? Or is reality merely fantasy in another guise? Certainly, when he built Disneyland, the first theme park of its kind, fantasy *became* reality. He taught us that even in reality, we are always on the periphery of fantasy, if we only choose to believe.

He touched our lives whether we lived in big cities like Philadelphia, Pennsylvania, or stick towns like Corbett, Oregon. He showed us that we really do live in "a small world after all" and even now, more than thirty years after his death, we still cling to Walt Disney and his ideals. He continues to serve as a source of joy and inspiration to the child in all of us.

Walt's optimism stemmed from his unique ability to see the whole picture. The key to his extraordinary vision was that he was as grounded in his memories of yesteryear as in his dreams of tomorrow. A history buff, he never turned his back on the past, because to him it was the foundation of the future. As a result, Walt Disney never threw technology at us piecemeal, but instead wove his inventions into a beautiful tapestry that supported his self-appointed mission to enhance our quality of life. To him, every invention was a valuable piece of a puzzle, and as a master communicator, he presented the future to us in a way we could grasp without hesitation. Walt was our bridge from the past to the future.

For those fortunate enough to know and work with Walt Disney, he remains unforgettable. They say he influenced who they are, how they think, and how they work. He changed their way of being.

But, those who "knew" Walt also say he was a hard man to *know*. Enigma is a word frequently chosen to describe him. Who was he and what made him tick? Some excellent biographies exist, as well as some ludicrously inaccurate accounts of his life, which rank as little more than bad fiction.

We can never really know who Walt Disney was because he was so many different things to so many different people. The firsthand observations in this book from those who knew, loved, and were in awe of him paint a vivid and compelling portrait of a remarkable and complex man. Some memories will jibe, while others conflict. He was, after all, human.

Through the eyes, hearts, and minds of those who were nearest to Walt, you will experience their frustrations with his impossible demands for perfection, their inspirations ignited by his unstoppable mind, their laughter at his corny sense of humor, their affection for him as a loving family man, and the tears they shed for him upon his unthinkable death. This book is a bridge from those who personally knew Walt Disney to those who know of him.

Walt knew people pretty well—he was a great psychologist. I've always said that if you get forty people in a room together and ask each one of them to write down who Walt was, you'd get forty different Walts.

ROY E. DISNEY
NEPHEW/VICE CHAIRMAN OF THE WALT DISNEY COMPANY

HIS

PRIVATE

WORLD

WALT DISNEY was an enigma. A very public man, he was also intensely private. He kept his family life separate from Hollywood and yet his hobbies and amusements almost invariably dovetailed with his work. He traveled the world, but preferred to be at home. He stayed in the fanciest hotels, yet ate the simplest food. He hired the best artists and craftsmen, but he couldn't resist doing his own hands-on experimenting.

All who knew Walt agree that though it was brief, the most significant time in his life was the few years, ages five to nine, he lived in Marceline, Missouri. His life's work—drawing, animation, film, trains, Main Street at Disneyland, and more—all have roots deep in those green Missouri hills.

Walt doodled pictures of farm animals rather than do his school lessons. His knack for creating enduring original art forms took shape when he talked his sister Ruth into helping him paint the side of the family's house with tar.

Near the Disney family farm, the Santa Fe railroad tracks crossed the countryside. Often Walt put his ear to the tracks to listen for an approaching train, which might bring his uncle Mike Martin, an engineer who worked the route between Fort Madison, Iowa, and Marceline. Walt later worked a summer job with the railroad, selling newspapers, popcorn, and sodas to travelers. During his life, Walt would try to recapture the freedom he felt aboard those trains by

first building his own miniature sets, then creating a 1/8-scale backyard railroad, the *Carolwood Pacific* or *Lilly Belle.*

Walt discovered his first movie house along Marceline's Main Street. There he saw a dramatic black-and-white recreation of the crucifixion and resurrection of Christ which planted a seed.

During those carefree years in the country, young Walt also gained a love and appreciation for nature and wildlife, family and community, which were the foundation of agrarian life. Though his father could be stern and often there was little money, Walt was buoyed by his mother's humor and the support of his older brother, Roy, who later became his business partner and greatest benefactor.

After the family moved to Kansas City, Walt continued to develop his inherent talent for drawing. He also had a yen to act and perform. At school, he began entertaining his friends with imitations of his silent screen hero Charlie Chaplin. At his teacher's invitation, Walt would tell his classmates stories, while illustrating on the chalk-board. Later, against his father's wishes, he would sneak out of the house at night to perform comical skits at amateur contests in local theaters with his best friend Walter Pfeiffer.

By sixteen, Walt quit school and went to France with the American Ambulance Corps. Upon his return, he pursued a career in commercial art that soon led to experiments in animation. He began producing his own animated shorts for local businesses in Kansas City. By the time he began producing *Alice's Wonderland*, which was about a real girl and her adventures in a world of animated characters, Walt ran out of money and his company, Laugh-O-gram, went bankrupt. Rather than give up, however, Walt packed his cardboard suitcase and with his unfinished print of *Alice's Wonderland* in hand, headed for Hollywood to start anew. He was not yet twenty-two.

The early flop inoculated Walt against fear of failure; he risked it all three or four times in his life. It was Walt's optimism and faith in self and others that took him straight to the top of Hollywood society.

Still, he wasn't your typical Hollywood mogul. Rather than hang out with the who's who of the entertainment industry, he was more often home having dinner with his wife, Lillian, and daughters, Diane and Sharon.

In fact, socializing was a bit of a bore to Walt. Usually he dominated conversations and held his listeners spellbound as he expounded on his latest dreams or ventures. Those who felt closest to Walt were those who lived with him, his ideas, or both.

For work, he would gladly have dinner with a new director signed to one of his motion pictures, play polo with some of his artists, or invite one of his contract players out to his house to ride his backyard railroad.

Walt rarely showed emotion, though he did have a temper that would blow over as quickly as it blew up. At home he was demonstrative and affectionate. He gave love by being interested, involved, and always there for his family.

Probably the most painful time of Walt's private life was the accidental death of his mother in 1938. After the success of *Snow White and the Seven Dwarfs*, Walt and Roy bought their parents, Elias and Flora Disney, a home near the Studio. Less than a month later, Flora died of asphyxiation caused by a faulty furnace in the house. The guilt and grief haunted Walt the rest of his life.

Ultimately, Walt was a rugged individualist, who wasn't out to please anybody but himself. He was too busy creating, learning, and expanding to bother trying to impress people. Although he *did* impress them with his genuine enthusiasm and spark of life.

roy o. disney BROTHER

Back in Missouri, we had an old country doctor and neighbor—Dr. Sherwood. Walt drew a picture of the Doc holding the halter rope of his prize stallion. Doc gave Walt a quarter for the drawing and that was the highlight of Walt's life.

walter pfeiffer SCHOOL CHUM

On Lincoln's Birthday, Walt came to school all dressed up like Lincoln. He had a shawl that I guess he got from his dad. He made this stovepipe hat out of cardboard and shoe polish. He purchased a beard from a place that sold theatrical things. He did this all on his own. Principal Cottingham saw him and said "Walter, you look like Lincoln. Why are you dressed this way?"

Walt said, "It's Lincoln's birthday and I want to recite his Gettysburg address." He had memorized it. Walt got up in front of the class and the kids thought this was terrific so Cottingham took him to each one of the classes in the school. Walt loved that.

ruth beecher SISTER

On Saturday nights, we were always at the local movie house or "nickel show" as it was called. Sometimes there were vaudeville acts. One evening, to our family's surprise, Walt was taking part in a juggling act. He was the boy sitting in the top chair of a three-chair juggling act and I remember how very scared he looked.

dorothy puder NIECE

Walt was experimenting with early movies. He took movies of me walking down the sidewalk and dropping a milk bottle. Then he reversed the film and the pieces of the bottle came back together again.

roy o. disney BROTHER

He taught himself what he knew about animation. Walt got hold of some book, which became his Bible, and out of that he learned what he needed to know.

john cowles jr. FRIEND

Walt lived with us for a while in Kansas City. My father, Dr. J.V. Cowles, financed his first Studio, Laugh-O-gram. Walt was working at the Studio all the time. I used to stand behind him and watch him draw.

edna disney SISTER-IN-LAW

When we lived in Kansas City, Walt used to come out to our house. He was having kind of a struggle, financially, and when he'd get hungry he'd come over. We'd feed him a good meal and he'd talk until almost midnight about cartoon pictures, mostly, and things he wanted to do. He wasn't very old then—only about nineteen.

lillian disney WIFE

Here is insight into Walt: When he came out to Los Angeles from Kansas City, he traveled first-class on the railroad even though he was broke. He always went the best way.

roy o. disney BROTHER

Tomorrow was always gonna answer all of his problems. He was hanging around Hollywood and I kept saying, "Aren't you gonna get a job? Why don't you get a job?"

Walt could have gotten a job, but he didn't want a job. He'd get into Universal Studios on the strength of applying for a job, then he'd hang around the studio all day watching what was going on around the sets. MGM was another favorite spot where he could work that stunt. He had no intention of getting a job. He would have, as a last resort, while angling to make some cartoons.

I was in the hospital at Sawtelle recovering from TB, and Walt had sold somebody in New York on a series of pictures by correspondence. One night he found his way to my bed at eleven or twelve at night and shook me awake with the telegram of acceptance of his offers. He said, "Can you come out here and help me get this started?" So I left the hospital the next day and never went back.

virginia davis mcghee

Walt found a distributor for *Alice's Wonderland* and we packed up and moved to Hollywood. Walt's uncle lived there and he offered Walt room and board. His garage also served as a studio for Walt, where he created his animation. It wasn't a family enterprise as much as it was Walt's lack of money. He couldn't afford to hire a dog, so he used his uncle's police dog in films like *Alice and the Dog Catcher*. Walt would spin stories around whatever was available.

We'd film in a vacant lot. I would act in pantomime in front of a white tarpaulin that Walt would drape over the back of an existing billboard and along the ground. I would pretend that I was interacting with the cartoon characters that he indicated to me. Since they were silent films, Walt

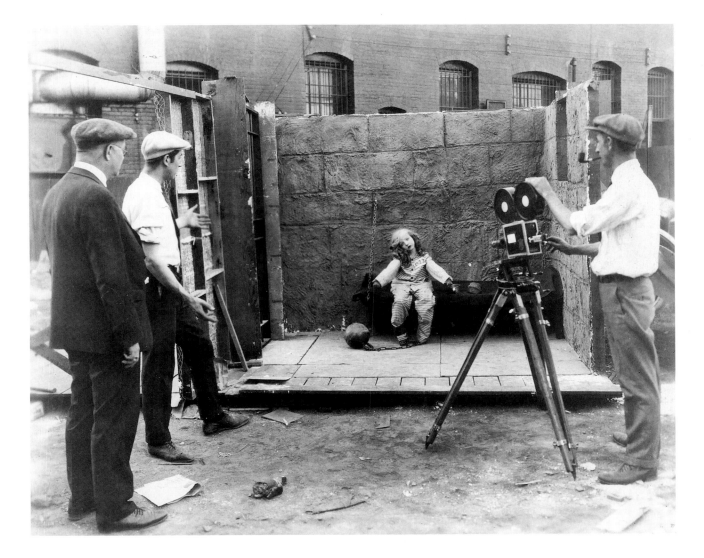

would direct me out loud, "Look frightened!" or "Sit down and pretend you're mad." With Walt, it was always "Let's pretend…"

Curious children from the neighborhood would act as playmates or extras in the live-action story and Walt would pay them each 50 cents. He kidded around a little with us, but he and Roy were under a great deal of pressure to meet demands and tight distribution deadlines. They worked very, very hard. They were the whole Studio crew—set makers, carpenters, cameramen, writers, and directors. Money shortages dictated that all live-action shots be completed in one take. Walt was always pleased with my performances even in just one take.

lillian disney   WIFE

When I first went to work for Walt, I made $15 a week. And sometimes he'd say, "Lilly, have you cashed any checks?" I'd say, "No," and he'd say, "Well, hold off for a while, will you?" So I'd keep them. I didn't need 'em. I'd put them away and he and Roy would use that little bit of money to pay their expenses.

roy williams   ANIMATOR

I was the fifteenth guy ever hired. I went to this little one-room building and a secretary said, "Walt will see you in a few minutes and you may go into his office"—which was nothing but a pile of junk in those days. I went in and waited. A traffic boy—just my age at the time—came in and shuffled some papers around and I got to talking to him about the weather and how I wanted to work for Walt Disney. We had a nice ten-minute conversation, then I said, "Maybe Mr. Disney is busy. I'd better come back another day."

The young man said, "I'm Walt Disney." I had some drawings in my hand and because I respected him so much based on what I had seen in his pictures, I just dropped them on his desk and blushed. He picked them up and held them over his face to keep me from seeing his smile. It was that closeness—in those few minutes when I thought he was a traffic boy—that made me and him become friends.

lillian disney WIFE

When he started taking me home from work then I began to look at him like he was somebody. He was embarrassed to stop in front of the house. One night he asked, "If I get a suit, can I come and see you?"

When he came to meet the family, he stood up and said, "Well, how do you like my suit?" My family liked him immediately. There was never any embarrassment about Walt. He met people easily. He was completely natural.

He was fun, even if he didn't have a nickel. We would go to see a picture show or take a drive up to Santa Barbara sometimes. He was always talking about what he was going to do. He always wanted to do the talking.

roy o. disney BROTHER

We roomed together for a while in Hollywood. It came to the point where Walt didn't like my cooking. He just walked out on my meal one night and I said, "Okay, to hell with you. If you don't like my cooking, let's quit this business." So I wrote my girl, Edna, in Kansas City and suggested we get married, which we did. Apparently, Walt didn't like living alone because he and Lilly were married three months later.

lillian disney WIFE

Walt always used to say I was such a bad secretary he had to marry me.

lillian disney WIFE

Marceline was the most important part of Walt's life. I remember when we used to take the train across country, he would drag people out in the middle of the night when we passed through Marceline. He had to show them where he grew up.

He didn't live there very long, but there was something about the farm that was very important to him. He always said apples never tasted so good as when they were picked off of the trees on the farm.

$\mathcal{T}$HE FAMILY MAN

roy o. disney BROTHER

Lilly was a kind of girl who let Walt have his way. She worshiped him and anything he wanted to do was all right by her. She had a lot of patience with him and they used to fuss at each other in their own kidding ways.

One time, they were in Colorado Springs driving around the countryside. Walt saw a sign "Petrified Trees for Sale." She didn't want to go in and stayed in the car. Walt found the owner and traipsed around. He was gone quite a long time and when he came back he knew she would be provoked with him.

It was near their anniversary so he said, "Honey, I bought you an anniversary present." She brightened up and said, "You did! What is it?"

"It's a petrified tree!"—a fallen tree that weighed some five tons. Officially, that was Lilly's tree and Walt had it shipped down to Disneyland.

sharon disney lund DAUGHTER

We weren't raised with the idea that this is a great man who is doing things that no one else had ever done. He was Daddy. He was a man who went to work every morning and came home every night.

diane disney miller DAUGHTER

The old witch in *Snow White* was our favorite game. It was "Play old witch with us, Daddy!" He maintained from experience with his own children that children love to be scared. And they do! He'd jump out from behind a door…we loved it!

He would blow up over little things. But when there was a crisis like a car accident, "Well, it's all right kid. We'll get another car." One time I skidded on a rainy street and bounced onto the curb into a palm tree. I was all shaken up. Dad couldn't have been more calm and understanding.

I must have been ten, the first time I remember any discord in our family. We used to always go to the Studio and have a big picnic with the personnel on the Fourth of July. One of the animators raised goats and had brought a kid to the picnic as a gift to us. It was a female, with a big red ribbon and bell around her neck.

When it came time to go home, Daddy put the goat in the car and Mother said, "We're not taking this goat home."

Daddy said, "What do you mean?"

"I won't have it," she said.

"Of course, you will," he said. "It's a gift for the children."

So he put the goat in the car and we were on the road home, when all of a sudden I heard this sobbing; Mother was sitting in the back seat, crying. It was the first time I'd ever seen her cry. These furious tears were just streaming down her cheeks.

Daddy got mad and said, "Okay. We won't keep the goat!" He took us home and headed back to the Studio with the goat. He spent half the night in his apartment at the Studio.

roy o. disney BROTHER

I remember one night Walt came down to my office. We sat from quitting time to eight or so and finally I said, "Look, Walt, you're letting this place drive you nuts. That's one place I'm not going with you," and I walked out on him.

I didn't sleep that night and he didn't either. The next morning, I was at my desk wondering what the hell to do. We were in a helluva tight fix—big payroll and everything. You don't worry about yourself, you worry about your commitments. I felt awfully low and heard his cough and footsteps coming down the hall. He came in and was filled up; he could hardly talk. He said, "Isn't it amazing what a horse's ass a fella can be sometimes?" and walked out. That's how we settled our differences.

tommie wilck WALT'S SECRETARY

I used to call the house every night when Walt left the office to let their housekeeper, Thelma, know that he was on his way home. This one particular night I hadn't called—I had forgotten.

Walt walked in the house and Thelma said, "What are you doing here?! Nobody called! Tommie didn't call!"

Then he went into the living room and Mrs. Disney said, "What are you doing here? We didn't know you were on your way home!"

He turned right around, picked up his hat and went back out. "That's a hell of a greeting when you get home! Is this my house or isn't it?"

diane disney miller DAUGHTER

He took us for drives after Sunday School. We'd go to Griffith Park almost invariably and play on the playground equipment and go on the merry-go-round for an hour or two or three. He never got tired. Sundays were so much fun and what made them so fun was that Daddy never got impatient with us. He wasn't hurrying us on like we do with our own children. He was just there enjoying us; he was *really* analyzing what we were enjoying and why.

sharon disney lund DAUGHTER

He was very understanding, but also stern. When he said no, he meant it. He didn't spank. All he had to do was raise that eyebrow and we knew...

lillian disney WIFE

Walt said I was the only person he could count on never to "yes" him. He had to have a sounding board. I had to listen carefully because when he had something he wanted to ask me, he would expect me to be listening.

diane disney miller DAUGHTER

Dad referred to his mother's death obliquely, but we never talked about it. I remember some years later, I was going through his drawers. He always kept an interesting collection of matchboxes and soap packages from hotels in them. In one of the drawers, I found a newspaper with the headline about his mother's accidental death.

sharon disney lund DAUGHTER

I took Daddy to work a couple of times. I remember driving down Sunset and asking him where his mother was buried and he said, "She's in Forest Lawn and I don't want to talk about it." Tears came to his eyes. Nothing more was said. He didn't believe in visiting her grave.

patty disney NIECE

Tom Jones, a Studio publicist, was assigned to take Walt to the Academy Awards one year. Walt told Lilly not to bother coming to the event because he didn't think he was going to win anything. So Walt went to the Awards and got so many that the press took photos of him holding all these Oscars.

When Tom drove Walt home, Lilly wouldn't let him in the house because she was so mad that he told her to stay home. She was furious because it had been a big night and she wasn't with him. So Tom had to drive Walt back to the Studio and he had to sleep in his apartment at the Studio that night.

19

"gee... another book... thanks a lot!"

"Boy! Only three days 'til Christ...

"Wow! Lookit those whiskers!"

"Ho... Ho... Ho!"

"...then this fat fella in a red suit says..."

"You mean Santa's coming tonight?"

Visions of sugarplums danced in their heads...

"Hello... North Pole... this is..."

"Santa, who?"

"Everyone hangs up a stocking... all I've got is a blue bootie!"

"I hear footsteps on the roof... I hope!"

"Not a creature stirring except Mickey Mouse!"

"...and I want a dolly, and a... "

"Humbug!"

"I am excited"

"It's nice... but what is it?"

Grandma and Grandpa Disney
Lilly and Walt
Wish you Seasons Greetings

diane disney miller DAUGHTER

Daddy never missed a father's function no matter how I discounted it. I'd say, "Oh Daddy, you don't need to come. It's just a stupid old thing." But he'd be there on time.

marjorie davis NIECE

He wore hats quite a bit. He would pick them up by the crown and put them on his head and Aunt Lilly would say, "Walt, fix that hat!" One time she took his hat off his head—that's when they had a convertible—and threw it out of the car. It went sailing. He stopped the car, went back and got it. He took one of his hats, made a heart shape out of the crown, had it bronzed and filled it with flowers for Aunt Lilly for Valentine's Day.

diane disney miller DAUGHTER

The day before Disneyland opened, my parents celebrated their thirtieth wedding anniversary. It began on the Mark Twain river boat with mint juleps and then moved over to the Golden Horseshoe Saloon for dinner and the "revue."

Suddenly Dad appeared in one of the balcony boxes on the side of the stage. At this point in the show, Wally Boag, as Pecos Bill, was firing blanks—Dad returned fire with his thumb and forefinger, then began to climb down to the stage. I think that everyone got a bit worried—I know I did. When he got to the stage he stood there beaming at everyone. He was so happy.

frank thomas ANIMATOR

Walt and Lilly had taken some dance lessons when the rumba or the mambo was just becoming popular. They came to a party where our band was playing. (Several of us, including Ward Kimball, formed a jazz band called The Firehouse Five Plus Two.) Walt came up and asked, "Hey, do you guys play that Bongo stuff? Lilly's been making me work on this new step—now we've got to see if I've got it down."

Then Walt took a spot back in the corner behind a palm tree. He was dancing stiffly and frowning and counting, "1, 2, 3, 4, 5, 6, 7, 8—1, 2, 3, 4, 5, 6, 7, 8..." He took it seriously; he didn't want to look like an idiot on the dance floor. He wanted to make Lilly happy because this was important to her.

diane disney miller DAUGHTER

He gloried in sentimentality. At my wedding, he was determined to make an issue of it. Ron and I were married in a little church up in Santa Barbara. Naturally, Daddy led me down the aisle and stood with me. I heard this sob, turned around, and Daddy was standing there with tears streaming down his cheeks. I squeezed his hand and he gave me a soulful look.

diane disney miller DAUGHTER

Our first child was going to be named Walter. But then when he was born, I felt I had to give him a new name—Christopher. Dad was very sweet about it, but said, "The next one is going to be Walter." We had three little girls after that. When the second girl was born, Dad was in Chicago and he sent a telegram addressed to Tamara *Walter* Elias Disney Miller. He was awfully cute.

ron miller SON-IN-LAW

Walt saw me play two games with the Los Angeles Rams and in each one I got injured. Once I got knocked unconscious and the other time, I tore my cartilage. After the season, he said, "You know, I've got three grandchildren by you. If you keep playing football, you're going to die and I'm going to have to raise those little guys." So he gave me a job at the Studio and I got out of football.

diane disney miller DAUGHTER

I remember Daddy telling my son Christopher, "Close your eyes and scribble." Then Daddy would take the scribble and turn it into a character.

$\mathcal{W}$ ALT AT PLAY

roy williams ANIMATOR

We used to play little softball games with Walt at the noon hour. One time the shortstop got the ball and kind of held it to let Walt get to first base. Walt stopped the game and said, "You treat me just like you would anybody else. You throw me out here at first. Let's play it honest!"

david swift DIRECTOR

We used to play badminton with him on the recording stage out at the Studio. We'd sort of feed shots to Walt because he wasn't much of an athlete. I don't know how he played polo. I didn't see how he could stay on a horse *and* swing a mallet.

marc davis ANIMATOR

There was an early time when Walt's social life was with the men that he employed—Freddy Moore, Norm Ferguson, Ham Luske—These men played badminton with Walt. They went up to his house when he lived in Los Feliz. Then when the Studio began to become really something, a few of these men weren't growing to the same degree that he was. So pretty soon his associations were mostly with people away from the Studio and his private life became divorced from the Studio. Many of these men never could understand that Walt had outgrown them—he had changed.

roger broggie MACHINIST

There was an accident and he stopped playing polo, gave his horses away, and had no hobby. His doctor told him he had to do something. So he started building this tabletop model train set with little billboards and trees. He assembled the train and laid the track. He built it for his nephew and gave it to him for Christmas. Then he said, "How 'bout a real one, now?" It started out as therapy for him; he wanted to keep busy with his hands.

ollie johnston ANIMATOR

I think it was Christmas of 1948. Ward Kimball came into my office and said, "Hey, Walt's got a Lionel train upstairs. Let's go see it."

While we were there, Walt came in and looked at me and said, "I didn't know you liked trains."

"Yeah," I said, "I got a backyard railroad."

And his exact words were "Hey, I always wanted a backyard railroad!"

So a couple of weeks later he came out to see my engine, while we were still building it. A few months later, he came out again and looked at the boiler and said, "That firebox door's too small. You'll have to put the coal in with an eyedropper. Mine's gonna be bigger!" and he made his engine a half-scale bigger than mine.

ward kimball ANIMATOR

At Walt's parties, I never saw him in old blue jeans. He always wore new blue jeans with big eight-inch cuffs with a straw hat and a beat-up plaid lumberjack's shirt. Right in the middle of one of his parties with Jules Stein of MCA, George Murphy, Louise Fazenda and Salvador Dali, we heard this damned circular saw going; Walt was in his barn shop working. I think he took delight in letting people know he was a common man. He'd come out once in a while and talk to the guests. He was like a little boy.

michael broggie SON OF DISNEY MACHINIST

Walt would walk through the Studio machine shop and say, "You guys are having all the fun. Why can't I get involved in this?" So the next morning the machinists put up a little sign that said, "Walt's bench." Walt walked in, saw this bench and without missing a beat, took off his coat and hung it up, grabbed an apron, tied it on and started going through the tools laid out on the bench. He looked up, and of course, everybody was waiting for a reaction. Walt, who was a consummate actor, said, "What the hell are you guys looking at? Haven't you ever seen an apprentice report in to work before? Come on, let's get to work. We've got a railroad to build!" With that everybody laughed and Walt became one of the guys in the shop.

frank thomas ANIMATOR

Walt always liked to do things with his hands. One of his hobbies was making miniatures, little stagecoaches and furniture, and he was very good at it. He grew up respecting people who could make things with their hands. He was impressed with skilled woodworkers and for some reason he always thought a carpenter ought to be called "mister." The only person he called mister at the Studio was a nice old fellow who could make anything out of wood. Walt called him *Mister* Rogers out of respect.

roger broggie MACHINIST

Ray Fox, a carpenter, taught Walt how to operate woodworking tools. Walt would go between the machine shop and the carpenter shop. The first locomotive he built was the *Lilly Belle*. He built its headlight and the smokestack, entirely. Then he said, "I'm going to build a caboose all by myself." He scaled blowups of photographs from historical records and built the caboose. He even photographically reduced a *Police Gazette* to scale and placed it into a magazine rack.

The department head asked me if I would show Walt how to run a lathe, drill press, and other machinery. It was hard to show Walt because he was impatient. I set up a lathe and turned out a piece and said, "That's how you do it." Then he turned the wheels and a piece flew out at him and he said, "Why didn't you tell me it would to do this?" (It's something you don't tell people; it's something they learn in the course of doing.)

Once, he said, "You know, it does me some good to come down here and find out I don't know everything." Still, you only had to show Walt once and he got the picture.

lillian disney WIFE

He really didn't have time to make friends. Sam Goldwyn was one, but we very seldom saw him socially. Walt had too much to do. He had to have a clear mind for work the next day.

dick van dyke ACTOR

On a couple of occasions, we went out to dinner with Walt and Lilly. It was like going out with your parents. They were maternal and paternal. He would say, "What do you say, Mother?" or "What do you want to have, Mother?"

lillian disney WIFE

When we built the Holmby Hills house, he had that train in mind. Walt took one look and said, "That's it!" He could see that train there.

herb ryman ARTIST

The tunnel of the railroad in Walt's backyard was 120 feet on a long "S" curve, so you couldn't see the other end when you were inside. Walt liked the mystery. The foreman on the job suggested it was cheaper to build it straight and Walt said, "It's cheaper not to build it at all."

diane disney miller DAUGHTER

When my sister and I were little, I remember going to the airport with Dad on Sunday outings and watching the planes come and go and the trains at the train station. He'd get down and listen to the track and make all kinds of silent observations.

ollie johnston ANIMATOR

A bunch of General Motors big shots were coming over to Walt's house to ride his train. I fired it up for him and then took it around on a test run. As I came across the driveway, kaboom! It went off the track! Walt came running over and said, "Shut it off! Don't let it dig a hole like a mole!"

He said, "You were going too fast!" and then pretended to get out a little notebook to list all of my mistakes.

"I didn't think I was," I said.

"Yes, you were!"

So I shut up and we put it back on the track and he said, "I'll take it around." He did and it went off the track at the exact same place. Then the gardener walked over and said, "Oh, I forgot to tell you, the truck backed over that part of the track."

Walt looked at me and said, "That lets you off the hook…but I still say you're a lousy engineer!"

lillian disney WIFE

Walt would never take a vacation. Once he announced he was going to take a week off and we would go to Santa Anita and watch the horse races every day, but he tired of that rather quickly.

ward kimball ANIMATOR

He'd say, "Let's put the train away and go up to the party house and I'll make chocolate ice cream sodas." He'd get behind the counter of his soda fountain, which was his boyhood dream come true with all these different flavors of ice cream, and he'd make these big tall things with whipped cream and cherries. They'd be a mile high and he'd bring them to Jules Stein or whoever his guests were. He was excited because he was doing something he liked to do.

marc davis ANIMATOR

Just before Walt went on a trip to Europe, he visited Sal the Barber at the Studio.

He asked Sal, "Can't you do something so I'm not as easily recognized?"

Sal looked at him and said, "Let me cut off your mustache."

And Walt said, "I don't want to look that different!"

joe grant STORY ARTIST

Walt was a very good traveling companion although he was kind of sour in the morning. Talk about *companion*! During flights on those old airplanes, I would sit there white-knuckling it and Walt would be fast asleep. He used to take Seconal before he got on the plane, so at every stop in the snow and ice I was dying and he was sound asleep.

bob gurr IMAGINEER

After a business lunch in Pittsburgh, we went to the Sheraton Hotel and Walt said, "That was a terrible lunch. I'm hungry! Let's go in the coffee shop and get a cheeseburger." As we walked in, there was a little drugstore section of the shop where Walt spied some Disney merchandise on a bottom shelf. He said, "Come on boys…" and started clearing the top shelf, while we were down on our hands and knees pulling out the Disney merchandise and handing it up to him to place on the top shelf. A saleslady came over and asked, "May I help you gentlemen?" (She didn't recognize Walt.)

"No," said Walt. "We're all right. We'll have this done in just a few minutes…"

ward kimball ANIMATOR

While in Chicago with Walt, he asked if there was any place I wanted to go. I told him of a jazz group playing someplace and he said, "You can do that anytime. Let's go ride the El." So we rode the damned elevated train half the night and he was looking out the window, reliving his childhood.

kelvin bailey WALT'S PILOT

One morning, in San Antonio, we met for breakfast in
our hotel by the waterway, when out of the blue Walt asked
the waiter, "Will you please call the manager?" So the
manager came over and Walt said very graciously, "I've been
looking at this room here. It's a nice dining room, but may I
make a couple of suggestions? You need to engender an
image of hospitality and if you were to change the design
here, make this archway round instead of square, add a coat
of blue instead of green, put a chandelier over here…" and
he began sketching his suggestions on a napkin. This went
on for about half an hour, and there were three or four
hotel staff taking notes.

A year later, I happened to visit that same hotel and
dining room, and guess what—it was just as Walt had
described, to detail! The manager told me the restaurant had
been a gold mine ever since.

lillian disney WIFE

On one of our last trips, we went to Williamsburg and
Charleston, and in Charleston, Walt knew more about the
sites than the guide.

diane disney miller DAUGHTER

One time when Mother and Dad were in London, the driver of their car told them there was a Disney Street in London. So the next day, they went with a photographer and had their picture taken there. Dad said it was a little tiny half street and he learned the history of it. Before it was Disney Street it had been called "Dung Hill Street."

ward kimball ANIMATOR

Walt called me and said, "Hey, Kimball, this is Walt!" That always bothered me because I knew other Walts, and I said, "Walt who?"

"Disney, for cryin' out loud. How'd you like to go to Chicago with me to see the railroad fair?"

So our wives saw us off at the Pasadena Station. Now this was the Santa Fe Super Chief, the real fancy train, and of course, the dining car steward knew Walt was aboard that train. He shuffled in and started telling us about the specials they were having for dinner.

Walt asked me, "What are you having?" I was looking forward to one of the best dishes I had ever tasted and that was the beef stew, cooked railroad style. They had a way of kind of burning the meat—delicious! So Walt ordered the filet mignon and when I ordered the Santa Fe Beef Stew, he looked at me and said, "Beef stew?! What do you want that for? Bring him the filet!" So I had the steak and that was that.

bill cottrell STORY ARTIST

Walt was a tourist. He had a feeling that if something was there, like the Statue of Liberty, it's there for a reason and you ought to go see it.

bill cottrell STORY ARTIST

We were traveling through New England and had lunch at some little restaurant, where we saw a number of paintings by Norman Rockwell on the wall. Walt said to the waitress, "Norman Rockwell lives around here, doesn't he?"

"Yes," she said. "As a matter of fact, it's two or three miles across a covered bridge and on the left."

Walt had known or corresponded with Norman Rockwell so we dropped in on him, unannounced. He was happy to see Walt. We went to his studio and saw all the new paintings he was working on. That was a great afternoon.

card walker STUDIO EXECUTIVE

Walt didn't like the food over in London. So he'd bring chili and beans and other canned foods he liked to eat. At the Dorchester Hotel, where we always stayed, the waiters would serve him chili and beans and crackers.

diane disney miller DAUGHTER

On a ship in the middle of the ocean, Dad would go out of his mind. He couldn't find enough to do. On one trip, he got in a shuffleboard tournament with Catholic priests who were returning from a pilgrimage.

KIDS AND ANIMALS

roy e. disney NEPHEW

One of Walt's great lines was when our son Roy was born. He came over to St. Joseph's Hospital, and it was right in the heart of the Baby Boom and he was trying to pick our baby out from the crowd. He said, "Look at that! Seven years from now, they'll all be out there watching *Snow White!*"

dick may DISNEYLAND EMPLOYEE

One day, when I was working the rafts at Disneyland, Walt came through the area on one of his walks. As he was passing, a man recognized him, ran after and grabbed him by the upper arm. Before Walt could utter a word, the man literally dragged him over to where his wife and child were sitting. He said, "I want my kid to meet you." Walt knelt down in front of that little boy and made over him like he was the only child in the world.

diane disney miller DAUGHTER

He used to go over to the machine shop at the Studio at night and work on his train or miniatures. He'd take our dog, D.D. (Duchess Disney), with him. She was an old brown clod with no spark of life in her, but she was very lovable and understanding of Daddy. There came a time at night, however, when even D.D. wanted to go home. She'd nuzzle his knee and Dad would say, "Okay, D.D. Let's go home."

kurt russell ACTOR

Sometimes he'd come down to the set and ask, "Do you want to see part of a movie that's being put together?" So I'd watch a movie or parts of a movie with him and we'd talk about it and he'd ask me questions. What was interesting about Walt, as I look back on it now, is that he was picking the mind of an uninhibited thirteen-year-old. He would ask, "What do you think of this?" and we'd kick ideas back and forth. I think he was finding out how a young mind worked.

lillian disney WIFE

Walt wouldn't allow the gardener to set traps for the ground squirrels or gophers. He said, "They're little creatures and have to live like anybody else. They're not hurting anything." In the canyon, we had all kinds of fruit—strawberries, boysenberries, peaches—and wonderful cantaloupe that the squirrels would pull away from the vine and go in to get the seeds. Walt would say, "Let them have it. You can go to the grocery store to buy food, but they can't."

45

winston hibler PRODUCER

In the True-Life Adventure films, if there was humor in nature, Walt wanted to point it out in the narration. But when the humor used the animals as puppets or jokes, he didn't like that. He called that "talking down to the animals" and we couldn't do that.

jim macdonald VOICE OF MICKEY MOUSE

During a story meeting, this director said, "At this point, we'll have the narrator say, 'When all the kids get a new bike…'" Walt spoke up, "No! Too many kids will *never* get a bicycle, let alone a *new* one, and that will break their hearts!" He was very protective of children.

marie johnston WIFE OF ANIMATOR

Walt was up here to check out Ollie's railroad track and I was in the living room feeding my son a bottle. The phone rang and Walt grabbed both my son and the bottle from me so I could answer the phone. I came back to get him and Walt said, "No, no, no! We're doing fine!" Walt finished feeding him, put the towel over his shoulder and burped him. He knew just what to do.

harrison ellenshaw SON OF DISNEY ARTIST

My dad and I would often go down to the Park while it was under construction. One time, we were there walking along, when we saw Walt. He looked at me and said, "C'mon, over here." We walked over to the railroad tracks and he pointed at this handcart and said "Jump aboard." I did and he began pushing that heavy thing to get it up to speed. Then, huffing and puffing, Walt hopped on board with me and we rode that thing until it came to a complete stop. From a ten-year-old's point of view, it was amazing to see this grown man getting as big a thrill out of riding that flatbed as I was. I remember seeing this big grin on his face.

dick jones VOICE OF PINOCCHIO

On occasion, when there would be a lull in recording my lines, Mr. Disney would take an old storyboard drawing, pin it up on a 4 x 8 celotex sheet and start a dart game with me, using pushpins. He was good at throwing pushpins, underhand, and making them stick with fantastic accuracy…he always won the game.

jim macdonald VOICE OF MICKEY MOUSE

Mary Flanagan had the concession at the Studio. Walt came in for a cup of coffee and sat at the counter. He didn't see it, but this maverick dog wandered in just behind him. Then he noticed the dog and Mary said, "I'll have to call the guard, I don't know where this dog came from." Walt said, "He's probably hungry. Give him a hamburger."

So Mary gave the dog a hamburger—and Walt had his coffee. Walt put his dollar down and Mary gave him forty cents change. He yelled "What kind of price are you charging for coffee, Mary?"

She said, "The coffee's only a dime, Walt, but the dog was your guest and that was fifty cents for the hamburger." He took the forty cents and chuckled as he left.

BY MOST definitions, Walt Disney was a workaholic. After dinner at home, he would usually read a script or review materials for the next day. He would go to bed early, only to wake up in the middle of the night with an idea. Rather than roll over and go back to sleep, he would get up, light a cigarette and head for his bedroom worktable to sketch, write and develop his dreams.

Walt's interests shifted over the years. During the 1930s, he focused on transforming the animated film from a series of plotless gags to a unique storytelling art form, beginning with *Snow White and the Seven Dwarfs*. During the forties, he was preoccupied with a cartoonists' strike followed by World War II. The fifties brought Walt renewed vigor and inspiration as he developed Disneyland and produced live-action films, as well as programs for an up-and-coming medium—television. In the sixties, like most of America, his focus turned to the social realm. Concerned with problems in society, he sought to harness technology and enhance the American way of life. He envisioned EPCOT, his experimental prototype community of tomorrow, as a working laboratory in which to test his ideas and technology. Around the same time, he also began conceiving California Institute of the Arts, better known as CalArts, which would provide a new kind of art education.

Walt's workdays were always exhausting. He left home around 7:30 a.m. When his daughters were young, he drove them to school. Once he dropped them off, his short trip to the Studio was the only chance he had during the day to be alone with his thoughts, ideas, and plans.

His office consisted of two rooms—one with a traditional desk arrangement for formal occasions, another with a coffee table and comfortable living room furniture where he did most of his work. Walt's longtime secretary, Dolores Voght Scott, was stationed outside of his office and controlled access to the inner sanctum. Tommie Wilck joined his staff in 1960 and he referred to her as his "secretary of the exterior." When Dolores retired in 1964, Lucille Martin came aboard as Walt's second assistant.

Another major player in Walt's working world was Hazel George, the Studio nurse who served as his confidante and sounding board. Walt would regularly go to Hazel's office for treatments for an old polo injury. He would climb into a traction harness to stretch his neck and receive compresses to relieve the chronic pain. After five p.m. each day, she was called to his office to massage his neck, help him deal with a variety of physical ailments and unwind from the stress of the day. Hazel was a source of Studio gossip and lively conversation.

Stories of Walt prowling Disneyland early in the morning or the Studio late at night are legion. He did not see his Studio inspections as an invasion of artists' privacy, but a way of preparing himself for story meetings.

Walt surrounded himself with the very best artists, storytellers, craftsmen, and filmmakers. As a boss, he was capable of lifting their talents to unimaginable heights, often exceeding even their own wildest imaginations. He was also a tough taskmaster who instilled fear and frustration. Despite his moods and occasional harsh outbursts, he was loved and respected by the majority of his staff. Some saw him as a benevolent dictator and paternal figure. Others, who didn't share Walt's vision, usually left the Studio or found themselves with lesser assignments until they finally decided to move on. By most accounts, Walt was demanding but not unreasonable; temperamental but caring. Like all humans, he had his share of flaws, but compared to the other Hollywood moguls, Walt was a saint.

During the 1930s, Walt was focused on transforming animation into a more significant art form. Not only did he push his animators to enhance the quality of animation and believability of characters, but he demanded superior storytelling.

He first improved the storylines of his animated shorts using a new device called storyboards, which enabled the team to work out the entire story in advance of production.

By 1937, Walt realized his dream of creating a full-length animated feature that could move audiences to not only laughter, but tears. *Snow White and the Seven Dwarfs* won an Academy Award, which was presented to him by child star Shirley Temple.

The early 1940s were troublesome. In May 1941, a faction of Studio artists entered into a divisive and protracted cartoonists' strike. Walt was against unionizing for a number of reasons, primarily because he felt he treated his staff fairly and didn't want any outsiders arbitrarily telling him how to run his company. The rapid growth of the Studio complicated the situation. The personal relationships the artists shared with Walt suffered as the Studio expanded to more than two thousand employees.

Eventually, Walt's brother Roy worked out a settlement while Walt was on a goodwill tour of South America on behalf of the U.S. government. The Studio ultimately accepted the union's demands but the impact on Walt was devastating. He would never again have the same relaxed and informal relationship with his artists.

The war years were filled with stress and financial trouble. Even before America entered into the conflict, the war in Europe had cut into a major portion of the Studio's overseas revenues. Then, the day after the attack at Pearl Harbor, the U.S. military commandeered the Studio lot, transforming its soundstage and parking sheds into automotive maintenance and ammunition storage facilities.

Walt readily supported the war effort by producing animated training and propaganda films for the government, which accounted for 93 percent of the Studio's overall production. Training films did not feature Disney characters, but graphics, stop-motion, limited animation, and diagrams, which educated U.S. servicemen on subjects ranging from how to identify aircraft to how to prevent malaria. The propaganda films he produced for the government further cut into the Studio's waning revenues. Such films as *The New Spirit* (1942) were provided free of charge to theaters and as a result, orders for regular Disney animation were canceled. Additionally, nearly one-third of Walt's artists were drafted, while the Studio's overall production jumped from 30,000 feet of completed film a year to 300,000 feet a year.

After recovering from the demands of war, Walt embarked on two new adventures: theme parks and television. By the mid-1950s, he began appearing on television to promote his imaginative Disneyland; his name again became a household word. During this time, Walt

also realized a lifelong goal to produce live-action films, beginning with *Treasure Island* in 1950.

It was a decade of renewed creativity and innovation for Walt. Relying on his uncanny instincts, he plucked artists and designers from one area of the company and transplanted them to others. It was not unusual for animators to suddenly find themselves designing attractions for Disneyland at WED (Walter Elias Disney) Enterprises, Walt's design and development organization, today known as Walt Disney Imagineering. Walt also enlisted an ex-navy admiral (Joseph Fowler) and, later, a retired army major general ("Joe" Potter) to help accomplish his daunting tasks of building theme parks.

In the 1960s, Walt scored successes in movie theaters (*Mary Poppins*) and on television (*Walt Disney's Wonderful World of Color*) and with popular new attractions at Disneyland, beginning with The Matterhorn in 1959. The New York World's Fair in 1964-65 gave him an opportunity to test the waters for an East Coast theme park and to research and design concepts for such technology as Audio-Animatronics. During that period he also purchased 27,500 acres of land near Orlando, Florida, and his plans for a theme park and EPCOT were officially announced.

Around the same time, Walt was also developing CalArts. As the father of "infotainment" or "edutainment," he had already successfully created films that both educated and entertained. Shifting his focus from film to the classroom, he envisioned a new kind of school where artists of all kinds—animators, actors, musicians, and more—would congregate, influence and learn from one another.

Sadly, Walt was forced to entrust CalArts and EPCOT to those with whom he had worked. Upon his death in 1966, he left behind many unrealized dreams.

hayley mills ACTRESS

It must have been 1959 when I first met Walt. Me, my parents, my younger brother, and our white Pekinese dog named Suki went to see him in the Harlequin Suite at the Dorchester Hotel in London. He wanted to meet me because he was interested in casting me as Pollyanna. I remember Walt and I were crawling around on the floor after the Pekinese, who was eating potato crisps on the carpet. Walt thought the Pekinese was wonderful! I wasn't nervous about meeting Walt. I was more concerned, really, that the Pekinese might pee on his carpet because she wasn't yet housetrained.

shirley temple black ACTRESS

As a child, I saw most everybody from belt level. As a result, I became a connoisseur of hands, belts, and shoes, since faces were usually pretty far up there. Walt's hands looked like those of an artist.

annette funicello MOUSEKETEER

I first met Walt on my audition for *The Mickey Mouse Club*. I was such a fan of his and I was scared to death, but his demeanor was so lovely and comforting.

He said, "Can you sing us a song?"

I said, "No. I'm sorry, I don't sing."

"Surely you can sing something," he said. So I did and I was so relieved when I sang my last note of the torch song "That's All I Want from You." I could see a smile on his face.

richard sherman SONGWRITER

The Studio needed a song for Annette Funicello to sing in *The Horsemasters*. We demonstrated "Strummin' Song" for Jimmy Johnson and he said, "That's very nice. Now, Walt's got to hear it."

"Walt who?" We didn't dream we'd have to see Walt Disney. As we walked into his office, Walt was sitting behind his desk signing photographs. His opening line to us was, "So are you really brothers?" Then he said, "Let me tell you about this picture" and he started describing *The Parent Trap*!

After a few minutes my brother Bob said, "Mr. Disney. We came to play you a song that we wrote for Annette to sing in *The Horsemasters*."

"Whoa! Why did you let me go on like this?" he grunted. "Come with me" and we walked into a second office where there was a piano. After I was through singing "Strummin' Song," he said, "Yeah, that'll work. Now, look, take this script home, *We Belong Together* (which was the working title of *The Parent Trap)*. There's a couple of places for a song. I don't like this title, maybe you can come up with a better one."

He basically threw us out of his office and we felt as though we had just been kicked. All he said about our song was "That'll work!?" I mean, what kind of a compliment is that? So we staggered out and Jimmy Johnson was bursting at the seams. "Oh, my God, what a meeting!" he said. "Walt accepted one song and he's given you a feature. This is unbelievable!" It was unbelievable.

sherry alberoni MOUSEKETEER

The very first time I met Walt was at the press opening of Disneyland. I was not a Mouseketeer then. I was a Bluebird for the Junior Camp Fire Girls and had sold more candy than any other girl in the state of California. My prize was to represent the Bluebirds at Disneyland and to make an ice cream sundae for Walt Disney at the Carnation Café on Main Street.

It was a really hot day and they had me standing on an apple crate because I was real short. The photographers were taking pictures of us and they kept yelling, "Just one more shot, just one more..." Mr. Disney and I were holding on to the ice cream sundae and smiling for the cameras, while the sundae was melting all over the sleeve of his suit. He was good-natured about it though. He wanted to make sure the photographers got the shots they needed at the cost of a suit cleaning.

mary costa VOICE OF SLEEPING BEAUTY

Late in the afternoon, there was a phone call. My mother answered the phone and it was Walt. He asked to speak to me. "Mary, I've chosen you to play the part of Sleeping Beauty. I'm confident you'll do well and that you'll be happy doing it. I hear something in your voice that is full of enthusiasm and I look forward to working with you. I won't be seeing you in sessions, but I'll be speaking to you on the phone."

That was our first conversation; most of our relationship was over the phone. His voice was extremely interesting to me. I could always tell Walt Disney's unusual voice.

By the time I met him in person, it seemed like I'd known him because we had talked so many times by phone. He came on to the soundstage and it was just like meeting an old friend because when you looked at him, his eyes appeared to be plugged into sockets, he was so bright.

hycy engel hill WALT'S FLIGHT ATTENDANT

I was hired as flight attendant for the Disney plane in March 1965. I met Walt when we flew to New York to pick him up and bring him back to California.

About ten or fifteen minutes before we expected him to board the plane, I heard somebody come bounding up the steps of the airplane into the cabin. It was Walt. He stuck out his hand to me and gave me a robust "Hi! I'm Walt Disney" and we shook hands. Now think about it: There I was working on *his* airplane; he had every right to assume that I knew who he was.

bob broughton CAMERA EFFECTS ARTIST

I met Walt on my very first day working at the Studio in the traffic department, delivering mail. I had been instructed that everybody was on a first name basis, even Walt.

So I was walking down the hall when here came Walt Disney. As we passed, I said "Hi, Walt!" and he went by me like I wasn't even there. I thought, I'd been set up and fell right into it.

A little while later, I was coming back down that same hall when here was Walt again. I was not quite bright, but I wasn't stupid, so that time I just looked straight ahead like there was nobody there. Just as I passed him, Walt grabbed me by the arm and said, "What's the matter? Aren't we speaking?"

Later, I learned that when Walt was working on a project, he was absolutely, totally serious. We used to say he had "tunnel vision" because when he was on a project, that's all he saw.

dick van dyke ACTOR

I was called to meet him about *Mary Poppins* and found out why everybody called him Uncle Walt. He was the most old-shoe guy I ever met in my life. He was comfortable to be around. An avuncular personality is what he was.

THE BOSS: TALES OF MOTIVATION, INSPIRATION AND FRUSTRATION

annette funicello MOUSEKETEER

I respected Walt so much. When I was first diagnosed with multiple sclerosis, of course, my family was foremost in my mind. Although I also thought, "If Mr. Disney were here, I could ask him what I should do. He would know."

herb ryman ARTIST

I look upon Walt as a conductor of one of the world's greatest symphonies, and I was part of the orchestra.

bob moore ARTIST

As I was leaving a meeting, Walt was standing by the door. It was a good chance to talk with him for a second and I said, "Walt, I'm sure you don't remember, but I'm a second-generation Disney employee. My father was a musician who recorded music for *Steamboat Willie.*"

"No," he said, "it was *Plane Crazy.*"

james haught jr. DISNEYLAND EMPLOYEE

Walt came into the warehouse one day smoking a cigarette and this new fellow instructed, "I'm sorry, sir, there's no smoking in the warehouse."

"Who said?" Walt asked.

"Walt Disney," the fellow said, not knowing who he was talking to.

"That's good enough for me," and Walt put his cigarette out.

lucille martin WALT'S SECRETARY

I couldn't keep from calling him "sir." I would answer the intercom, "Yes, sir."

And he'd say, "Yes, Walt."

The next time it would be "Yes, sir," and he'd correct me again, "Yes, Walt." Finally, he gave me this little cartoon drawing that said "Down with Sir!" I had it taped on my intercom until the day he died.

kurt russell ACTOR

The script lady pulled me aside one day and said, "I think they're going to offer you a contract. Do you know why Walt likes you? Because you're not intimidated by him." I never could figure out why anybody would be intimidated by him.

jack speirs WRITER

We were in a story meeting and Joe Rinaldi said, "You know I think we ought to use my son Riley in here, Walt. He'd be good."

Walt said, "Don't you think you're doing a little bit of nepotism here, Joe?

"Well, gee, Walt, I don't know. He's good." Then a couple of minutes later Joe said, "I have to go to the bathroom," and left.

Walt said, "Joe's going to look up 'nepotism' in the dictionary and find out if he's in trouble or not."

jim macdonald VOICE OF MICKEY MOUSE

One day, when the Studio was right in the middle of work on *Mickey and the Beanstalk,* I got a call directing me to see Walt immediately. When I got to his office, Walt said, kind of thoughtfully, "Jim, the animators are screaming for Mickey's dialogue. But I just don't have the time to do it. I don't know if I'll ever have the time to do Mickey's voice again." Then Walt surprised me with this question: "Ever do Mickey's voice? Try it!" So I did. We recorded an A and a B track, one with Walt doing Mickey and one with me doing it. Then we compared the voices and Walt said, "Sounds good to me!" Right then we switched over to using my voice for Mickey.

Some years later, I was on the stage recording Mickey's voice and Walt was in the booth. He got up to leave and called out to me with a big smile, "You know, I do Mickey too."

dick nunis THEME PARK EXECUTIVE

I was giving this pitch to Walt and he was just killing me. He said, "Nunis, you don't know what you're talking about," and walked out of the room. Everybody followed him and I sat there in this big room all by myself. I thought I had been fired and was thinking of where I could go to get a new job when I heard the door open behind me. It was Walt. He put his hand on my shoulder and said, "Look, young fella, you keep expressing your opinions; I like it."

I think he tested people. Later, I would sit in meetings and watch him take a position and see who would go with him. Then he would take the opposite position and see who would go with him. I think the people who stuck to their guns, whether they were right or wrong, were the people he respected the most.

rosie shrode STUDIO COOK

I used to come to work at the Studio in the morning and he'd be riding around in his little surrey car and pull over and say, "Hop in, Rosie, I'll take you up to the time office."

peter ellenshaw ARTIST

He'd fill you with fire. I always tried to understand how he made me feel so good. It was magical really. He said one time he was "the bee that pollinated the flowers," but he didn't do it in a way you might think, like, "Oh, Peter, this is coming great! Oooh! *Very* good!" He'd never say anything like that. He'd talk about the project rather than how good or bad you were doing. He inspired you to create what *he* wanted.

kevin corcoran ACTOR

Sometimes I'd end up in his office when a new project came up. Walt would tell me about my next film role. Then he'd tell me the story and would just come alive as he described it to me. First, he was telling me about it, and then he was going to tell the world.

ollie johnston ANIMATOR

Walt was always prodding or needling people to improve their work. When I started on *Snow White,* I was an assistant to a brilliant animator, Freddy Moore, but Walt kept riding him hard to keep improving.

I animated one scene of Grumpy, and Walt seemed to like it. I'm certain he knew I animated it, but he asked Freddy, "Who drew this scene?" Freddy answered that I had done it and Walt said, "Be careful Fred, he's going to take your job!" It was Walt's way of pushing Freddy to work harder.

frank thomas ANIMATOR

When Fred Moore started animating the dwarfs, Walt made him do it over and over. He'd pick on the finger, the way Grumpy's eye worked and the little details. It wasn't so much that he was picking on Fred, he was sharing the experience with Fred. He knew he couldn't draw it and so he'd try to get Freddy to draw it the way he would if he could. They'd sit there and look at it in the sweatbox and laugh about it and he'd say, "Run it again. Let's see that one more time. You mind, Freddy? Hey, you know, what if you did…" and just pick, pick, pick, pick on the thing. But he did this because of his enthusiasm. And he did the same with story, color work, and everything else.

ollie johnston ANIMATOR

I caught the mumps from our kids and was laid up for four months. It affected my glands and I was so weak that I could hardly lift a glass off of the table. Walt carried me through. Every Thursday, Frank Thomas brought home my check. I wrote a letter to him saying I hoped to thank him by doing better work.

diane disney miller DAUGHTER

Dad wanted to take care of everybody. He wanted to know if an employee was sick or needed something. He knew about everybody's personal lives. Paternalism shouldn't always be a bad word: I think a lot of us like to know that someone cares about our well-being.

annette funicello MOUSEKETEER

Because I was so shy I wanted to see someone who might help me step out of my shell. I asked Mr. Disney if I could see a psychologist and he said no.

"People are attracted to you because of your shyness," he explained. "If you were to change that, then you wouldn't be you!"

cubby o'brien MOUSEKETEER

He used to come onto the set whenever one of us would have a birthday party. There would be a big sheet cake with a Mickey Mouse in the middle of it and we'd stop production and have a little party for about an hour or so.

Walt seemed to always have fun when he came down to the set at the birthday parties. There was never any tension when he was around. It wasn't like "Uh, oh, the boss is coming down…" We were always happy to see him.

kevin corcoran ACTOR

I was called to Walt's office, and while sitting there, he asked if everything was cool with me. He just wanted to make sure that as a little kid, I was happy doing what I was doing. That's the kind of boss he was.

jack speirs WRITER

Walt and Roy were debating one time whether or not to crack down on some artists because they were carrying all kinds of supplies out of the Studio and taking them home to do drawings.

Roy said, "We ought to put a stop to this."

And Walt said, "Nah. Don't stop them."

"But, Walt," Roy said, "you know they're selling their art." And Walt said, "Don't worry about it. We get the benefit. They're practicing. So let them go home and practice."

john hench ARTIST

I was working on an assignment that I didn't like—the "Nutcracker Suite" in *Fantasia*. I wanted to work on Stravinsky's "Rite of Spring." So I told Walt and he asked me, "Why do you want to work on that?" I said, "Because I don't know anything about ballet."

He said, "Wait a minute. I'm going to make a phone call."

The ballet was in town and he arranged for me to sit backstage for the whole season! That's what he wanted me to do, so I did. More than 150 drawings later, I learned something about ballet and worked on the "Nutcracker Suite" quite willingly.

annette funicello MOUSEKETEER

Walt asked me to make an appearance at Radio City Music Hall with the Rockettes and I said, "I'm graduating from high school, I can't go, Mr. Disney. Please don't make me go."

He said, "I promise you, you will have the best graduation ever. I won't let you down." So I did my six weeks with the Rockettes. On the night of my graduation, during our performance, the mayor of New York City presented me with my diploma, while the Rockettes were doing their famous kicks. It was spectacular!

winston hibler PRODUCER

You took the things Walt said and found something in them that inspired you. It was best to listen and not take notes with Walt. With a very few words, he could project creative thoughts and ideas that inspired people to create better. Walt in a single hour could transmit more ideas to a writer than I could in a whole day.

card walker STUDIO EXECUTIVE

The Studio's top publicity man, Joe Reddy, was a Democrat and would die a Democrat. There was nothing right but a Democrat. Walt knew that, so at any Republican function he didn't go to, he'd call Joe and say, "You go down and represent me." Joe used to hate that and Walt knew it.

tom wilck PUBLICITY CONSULTANT

You could sit and talk with the man and leave with another five great ideas that you wanted to pursue.

buddy baker COMPOSER

Walt came by and took a straight-backed chair and turned it around; he wanted to chat a bit. Finally, he said, "Have you had your vacation?"

"I haven't had time to take it yet. I've just been too busy with these projects," I replied.

"By God!" he said. "You take your vacation! I have time to take mine, and if I can take mine, you can take yours!" He didn't want us to suffer burnout. He ordered me to take a vacation and to tell the art directors to wait until I get back.

ben sharpsteen DIRECTOR

One time, when the squeeze was on, it was decided not only to lay off some unnecessary people, but maybe to reduce some salaries. However, Walt said, "I want a raise for certain men, my top animators; I want them to have higher salaries." Somebody remonstrated that it was not on the books. Walt said, "I can't make pictures without those people. I can't hire bookkeepers to draw pictures for me."

julie andrews ACTRESS

I would say he took a personal interest in my career. I don't know how much he personally cared, but I'm sure he was extremely proud that he had had the farsightedness to choose me to play Mary Poppins. I was nobody in the sense that I was only known on Broadway. I wasn't known anywhere else. But he treated me as if I was the most important star in the world.

john hench ARTIST

By the time you got your ideas back from Walt, you wouldn't recognize them as your own. He absorbed and digested everything. In the end, the production was all his.

jack speirs WRITER

After Ben Sharpsteen retired from the Studio, he bought a place north of San Francisco and Walt stopped in to check it out. It was a nice country place with a stream running along in front of the house and trees up on the hill and Walt said, "Ben, you could put a little dam down there in that stream and you'd have a nice lake out here and you can make a trail up to that forest up there, to those trees. Why don't you do that Ben?"

Ben said, "I've been waiting forty years to tell you this, Walt...*I don't want to.*"

chuck jones ANIMATION PRODUCER

I came to work for Walt in the 1950s, after Jack Warner produced a 3-D picture called *House of Wax*. When Jack suddenly realized they couldn't make 3-D animated cartoons, he fired the whole staff.

Trembling, I called Walt, and to my surprise he said, "Come on over!" I'd been at Disney a while when I noticed that nothing ever moved forward without Walt. You would make an appointment with him and six weeks would pass before he was able to get away from Disneyland and all his other projects. From my days at Warner, I was so used to working at breakneck speed that I finally realized Disney was not the place for me. So I went to tell Walt, who had been nice enough to bring me on. By that time, the Warner cartoon studio was up and running again and I had a mattress to fall on. Feeling brave, I said to Walt, "There's only one job at the Studio worth having…and that's yours."

Walt laughed and said, "Yeah, but it's filled."

fess parker ACTOR

When I'd say to Walt's secretary, "I'd like to see Walt if he has a moment," I don't remember anything except "Please go right on in." This was kind of a shock to me. After all, he was the head of the Studio. Quite often I'd find him in conversation with other people and he'd say, "Sit over there on the couch, Fess" or he'd simply motion for me to sit down and I'd wait until I could talk with him. He was always accessible.

T HE MAN BEHIND THE MOUSE: QUIRKS, QUALITIES AND CHARACTERISTICS

harriet burns ARTIST

Walt was famous for picking things up and knocking stuff over. He wasn't clumsy; he was interested—"What are you doing? Let me see?" One time, I was making little stained-glass windows for Storybook Land and had 369 pieces of cut lead placed in this tiny window, which I hadn't soldered together yet. Walt came in, picked it up and the lead went flying everywhere.

Another time, I was experimenting with polyester and I had a flit gun and was squirting water into the polyester to see if it would make lasting bubbles. Walt came in and said, "Let me try!" and snatched the flit gun out of my hands.

woolie reitherman ANIMATOR

Walt was the best salesman in the world because he felt he wasn't selling.

roy o. disney BROTHER

He had an eye that would grab yours when he was talking to you. If you'd waver or look around, he'd say, "What's the matter. Aren't you interested?" He wouldn't let go of your eye and that was his way of looking into you. You couldn't lie to him or say you liked something you didn't because it would show right in your eyes.

diane disney miller DAUGHTER

Complex? Well, yes and no. Dad was consistently what he was, which was semi-innocent and very directed.

julie andrews ACTRESS

I would describe him as a "twinkly person." He had a kind of cheerful merriment in his eyes. He didn't roar with laughter or anything like that, but there was a kind of bubbliness about him.

kurt russell ACTOR

He didn't blurt things out like a child. He sat and thought. I think he was a realistic dreamer. He was slower and a little more thoughtful and had an awareness about him; you felt like he was taking in the whole room.

joe grant STORY ARTIST

He was the sort of person that even when you came home at night, he was still walking around in your head. You could hear him.

roy e. disney NEPHEW

Bill Peet told me about how Walt just walked in one morning with half his mustache missing. It had been shaved off and Bill said he watched Walt walk by and wondered, "Should I mention this or not?" All he could conjure up in his own mind was "It was a horrible mistake and if I mention it to Walt, he's gonna kill me." So nobody ever mentioned it to Walt and it grew back over the course of the week.

dean jones ACTOR

In *That Darn Cat,* the Mercedes that Roddy McDowall drove belonged to Walt. Walt explained to me he was passing by a dealership and fell in love with that little two-seater, but it was $11,000!! He said, "I knew I couldn't afford that and I walked down the street, got more than two blocks away and said, 'Yes, I can afford it and I'm gonna buy it!'" So he went back and bought this little Mercedes, but felt so guilty about spending so much money that he started renting the car out for films. He got $100 a day for it on *That Darn Cat.*

frank thomas ANIMATOR

Lilly used to tell the story that when we had the first showing of *Snow White* at the old Studio theater, Walt said, "Hurry up, Lilly, we won't get a seat!"

She said, "At your own Studio, you won't get a seat!" This was the way his mind worked. He was so innocent and unsophisticated.

jim fletcher ARTIST

He was a lonely man and yet I don't think he was unhappy. He was happy because he was so successful. He thrived on his success. One time I asked him if he could do it all over again, what would he do? He said, "I'd do it all over again."

hycy engel hill WALT'S FLIGHT ATTENDANT

On one of our plane trips, I walked to the back of the cabin to see if Walt needed anything. It was kind of the wrong time to check on him; he was reading a script, sniffing, and tears were rolling down his cheeks. He looked up at me and was embarrassed. He was fumbling for his handkerchief and said, "How's that! A grown man like me can't even read a script without crying."

sharon disney lund DAUGHTER

He'd come into the house at night and we had this brown leather chair; it was Daddy's chair and the most comfortable chair in the world. He'd sit there with a script and when he read, he mouthed the words or lipped them. You could tell by his face when he was having a hard time with something in the script—an eyebrow would go up.

roy e. disney NEPHEW

He did not know how to delegate; that was probably Walt's biggest fault. I think it was probably what drove him to distraction in those last days because he couldn't let anything go by. Everything had to have his fingerprint on it somewhere. He would have to see it five times. You were insane to try to sneak something past him or not show it to him; he'd find out. We all believed he was omniscient.

joe grant STORY ARTIST

He didn't have an annoyingly big ego. I personally didn't resent his ego. He was better than anybody around there. He *was* the Studio.

roy e. disney NEPHEW

Patty and the kids were visiting the Studio one day and she parked our old Ford station wagon in Dad's parking place, which was right next to Walt's.

Walt left the Studio early that day. He got into his Mercedes 230 SL coupe, cranked the steering wheel, backed out and the front end of his car swung over and ripped the left side off of our new, used station wagon. Dick Kennon, who managed the Studio gas station at the time, heard the crash and rushed over to find Walt standing there, laughing his head off. Then Walt got back in his car and just drove away.

Dick told us about it later. I love the picture of Walt standing there laughing. I don't know if he knew it was our car or not. Of course, he didn't offer to pay for the damage and we never asked.

THE VISITOR

After the visit by the little old woman in the horse drawn wagon, Walt still seemed a little nonplused.

floyd norman STORY ARTIST

In the early 1960s, this little woman showed up at the Studio main gate in a horse-drawn carriage. It looked as though she had rolled off a movie set. She had traveled a distance to personally give Walt Disney a script. She pulled up to the main gate and said, "I want to see Walt Disney." Of course, the guards said, "You can't just show up and see him. He's a busy man!"

Word got up to Walt about this crazy little lady at the gate who wanted to see him. So he left his office, walked all the way out to the main gate, talked to her and then said, "Thanks for bringing your script. I'll read it!"

kevin corcoran ACTOR

Once a year, the John Tracy clinic for the hearing impaired would hold a bazaar to raise money. It was an organization that Walt supported and he would ask people under Disney contract to volunteer to put on a show, while he would help clear the tables. *Walt Disney* busing tables! It knocked my socks off when I saw that.

frank thomas ANIMATOR

Comic Strip Artist Floyd Gottfredson lived in Beverly Hills. One day he got a call at the Studio that his wife was sick and she was being taken to the hospital. So he told Walt that he was going to be gone for the rest of the afternoon and the first thing Walt said was "You got a car?"

"No."

"How will you get out there? Here, take my car," and he handed Floyd his keys.

diane disney miller DAUGHTER

Dad was very earnest, but he could contrive things too—little "cute-isms." I had read in several sources this story that my Dad told—"Walt asked his daughter Diane what girls her age would like to see in Disneyland, and she said, 'Boys.'"

I called Dad on that—"I didn't say that!"

"I know," he said, "but it's cute!"

81

charlie ridgway THEME PARK PUBLICIST

The day Walt went to the White House to receive the Freedom Award from President Johnson, he wore his Goldwater button inside his lapel. Walt had been terribly antipolitical until George Murphy ran for the Senate. Being a friend of George, he supported him and that got him into politics again. From then on he was a rather avid Republican. Johnson did not take Walt's political commentary with good grace at all.

diane disney miller DAUGHTER

I called him "corny" once when I was about fourteen years old and he responded, "I am and I'm proud of it."

joe grant STORY ARTIST

He had a peculiar walk. Since he was a farm boy, he looked like he was walking over furrows that had just been dug up. He had a kind of lope.

diane disney miller DAUGHTER

There were times even during my life when he was rather short of money although I was never aware of it at the time. There were always expectations that he was wealthier than he was. Dad was always investing in new dreams.

charlie ridgway THEME PARK PUBLICIST

Walt was always a little sensitive about his height. He looked to be taller on television than he was. He was particularly sensitive when he was standing with a group of people who were six feet tall or so. He would always get in the center of a group and kind of hold on to the people next to him and stand on his very tiptoes.

vernon scott JOURNALIST

He smoked too much. He was always smoking. He had nicotine-stained fingers.

diane disney miller DAUGHTER

You could always tell Dad's cigarette butts in the ashtray. They were about a quarter of an inch long and brown all the way through. He smoked 'em until he could barely hold them. He would forget to put them out. He would light them and get carried away with what he was thinking or talking about and just hold them. Sometimes he would hold them in his mouth or in his hand and get an ash on it two inches long. He forgot to smoke it. He would just hold it until it practically burned his fingertips.

lillian disney WIFE

We could never lose Walt. We could tell when he came home at night. If I was upstairs, I could hear him cough as he came through the gate. If we were in a crowd, I'd say "Well, where's Walt?" Pretty soon, I'd hear that cough and say, "Oh, yeah. There he is."

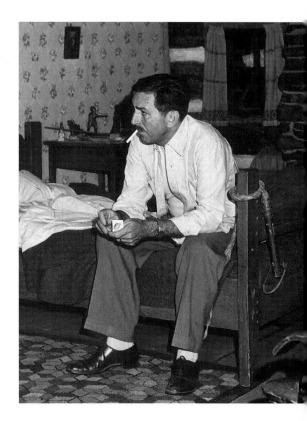

ward kimball ANIMATOR

I was right in the middle of describing a storyboard on a space show for television and he got into one of these coughing jags. It was longer than usual. It was embarrassing. I stood there and just blurted out, "For crying out loud, why don't you give up smoking?" Walt looked up, his eyes watering, and said, "A guy's got to have a few vices, doesn't he?" In other words, he knew damn well he ought to give up smoking. But he never did. I just blurted it out because I was kind of mad that here's this guy we all look up to and depend on and he's destroying himself.

sharon disney lund DAUGHTER

One of the people that Daddy really admired was da Vinci because da Vinci wanted to know how to make things work. One Christmas, Daddy was given a big book on da Vinci. He was fascinated by it. He spent all his Christmas afternoon reading that book.

ron miller SON-IN-LAW

The only time he'd sit still was when he had to read.

jack lindquist DISNEYLAND EXECUTIVE

He always called me Bob! I'd wear my name tag and everyone else called me Jack, but Walt called me Bob. One day Card Walker said, "You know, Walt, that's Jack, not Bob."

Walt looked at me, raised that eyebrow and said, "Looks like a Bob to me."

So the day we opened Small World, we had water from all over the world to dump in the trough. Then Walt and the chairman of the board of the Bank of America were in a parade together through the Park. Walt was supposed to attend a formal luncheon at the Plaza Inn. Before we ordered our meals, however, he said, "I'd like to stay for lunch, but Bob here has something for me to do. Aren't we late, Bob?"

I caught on and said, "Yes, sir, we'd better be going." We went behind the restaurant where the employees' cafeteria was. Walt gestured toward the Plaza Inn up front and said, "The food's just too fancy up there."

So "Bob" and the boss went in to the cafeteria together and had a bowl of chili.

diane disney miller DAUGHTER

He had an intensely religious youth. He'd been brought up in a strictly regimented church atmosphere. His father was a deacon at one time. I can understand why he had such a free attitude toward our religion. He wanted us (his daughters) to have religion. He definitely believed in God—very definitely. But I think he'd had it as a child; he never went to church.

bob thomas JOURNALIST

Driving back to the Studio from Disneyland with Walt, he talked the whole way. It was mind-boggling that he could continue this monologue without repeating himself.

tommie wilck WALT'S SECRETARY

Five o'clock was drink time in the office. If you were in the office at five o'clock, we always served drinks. Walt had a Scotch Mist and I always served whatever anybody else wanted.

The Scotch Mist is mostly ice. I would put ice and water in it and then float the scotch on top and not give him very much of it. He got the taste of the scotch without having had much of it. He may have consumed a lot of liquid, but I don't think he really got much liquor.

sharon disney lund DAUGHTER

Dad was careful about his image. He wanted kids to look up to him. He never let himself be photographed with a drink in his hand and I don't think too many photos exist of him with a cigarette.

diane disney miller DAUGHTER

When he gave gifts, he wanted to give something you would remember him by, like jewelry. He was afraid he was going to be gone and forgotten.

ollie johnston ANIMATOR

After we'd all gone home for the day, Walt would sometimes go through our work. We'd position our drawings in such a way, maybe turn them at a slight angle, so that we could tell if he'd been sifting through them.

marc davis ANIMATOR

Walt never complimented you to your face. You'd have a meeting with him and he'd say, "Yeah, let's meet again next week." Then an hour or so later, your door would open and some other animator would come in and say, "Boy, you sure did have a great meeting with Walt! I'd sure like to see the stuff you did." He'd told other guys how great your work was but he could never tell you personally.

ollie johnston ANIMATOR

Walt did compliment me once during *Pinocchio*. I was loafing outside his office talking to Ham Luske's secretary when he came walking down the hall and said, "Oh hi, Ollie! Hey, I sure like those Pinocchios you're doing."

"Whew!" I expected him to say, "What are you doing hanging around here?!"

All the secretaries were talking about the compliment he gave me and by five in the afternoon the entire Studio had heard about it. That was *big* news for an hour or two.

roy o. disney BROTHER

Talk about a memory like an elephant—Walt had one. He remembered when we left Chicago for the farm in 1906. My mother, my little sister, Walt, and I traveled by Santa Fe train. We stopped off at Fort Madison and while we were there, Walt found a pocketknife on the street. So just imagine, Walt was five years old and I was nine years older, so I took it away from him.

Sixty years later something came up at the Studio and Walt accused me of bullying him. He said, "You've been doing this to me ever since I was born! I remember you tried to take that pocketknife away from me!"

marty sklar IMAGINEERING EXECUTIVE

Walt asked a question in a meeting and I answered it. When I got back to my office I looked up the answer and learned I had given him the wrong information. I made a big mistake because I didn't call or send a note saying, "I gave you the wrong information. Here's the right answer."

A year later, a similar subject came up and I gave the right answer this time and he looked at me and said, "*Last time you said…*"

joe grant STORY ARTIST

He had an overwhelming power over people and the voice of a prophet. He was so damned intuitive. You always had the feeling he knew what you were going to say and he seemed to know things before they happened. That sort of omnipotence held a mental control over you. To gain his favor, people would do outlandish things.

I remember the time when television was on its way in and I said to Walt, "Why aren't we on TV?"

"Television will come to us," he said, and it did. He knew ahead of time.

bill anderson PRODUCER

A lot of people keep saying Walt wasn't a good businessman. Don't let anybody ever kid you that he wasn't. Roy never saved Walt from himself. They were a great team, however, Walt never went off into Never-Land without knowing where he was going.

milt kahl ANIMATOR

The first time I got a big raise (it was a helluva big raise) I thanked Walt for it, but he just got embarrassed. He acted like "Why aren't you down there at the drawing board where you should be instead of up here thanking me!"

floyd norman STORY ARTIST

Walt saw my gags about him; he even signed one. One of my gags came about during the civil rights movement, which was trying to force minorities into the Studio. The funny part was minorities weren't knocking at the gates to get in. The jobs were there if they wanted them and if they were qualified. It's like the old ruse that Walt didn't hire Jews, which was also ridiculous. There were plenty of Jews at Disney.

Personally, I never felt any prejudice from Walt. I got really upset at Spike Lee when he called Disney a racist. I said to myself, "Damn, Spike! You never even met Walt Disney!"

joe grant STORY ARTIST

He was *not* anti-Semitic. Some of the most influential people at the Studio were Jewish. It's much ado about nothing. I never *once* had a problem with him in that way. That myth should be laid to rest.

roy e. disney NEPHEW

Walt was Victorian prudish—that whole generation of our family was because that's the era they were from. One way it came out was in Walt's attitude toward death and sickness; there was something dirty about that sort of thing and it wasn't to be talked about.

harriet burns ARTIST

He was not a prude. When we made the mermaids for the Submarine Voyage, they had little boobs, and we said, "Of course, we'll cover these up with seaweed or something."

"No reason to," he said. "Nothing wrong with that."

roy o. disney BROTHER

Walt would never be outraged by competition. He probably would have taken the idea, revamped it, and used it in his next picture.

suzanne pleshette ACTRESS

I was just insane about him and everybody thought we'd hate each other because I'm somewhat bawdy. On the first day of filming *The Ugly Dachshund,* I had to fall in the water during the party scene. So I said, ingenuously, "Is it all right to have tits at Disney?" meaning, when I go in the water should I come up facing the camera or with my back to the camera because I was dressed in a white blouse. Walt had walked on the set and everyone was silent, thinking I was gonna be fired. Then Walt said, "Yes! It's all right. Face the camera!"

In another scene, the script said I had to fight with Dean (Jones) and then start to cry. I said, "My character wouldn't do that! She would kiss him and tease him to get her way." Walt asked, "What do you want to do?" I said, "I wanna kiss and tease him."

"You know," he said, "I can date the fall of the morality of the Studio to the day you walked on the lot."

lillian disney WIFE

Walt said about the Academy Awards that he was embarrassed to receive an award and he was embarrassed if he didn't get one.

ollie johnston ANIMATOR

Walt never grew up to the point where he couldn't appreciate something like a lullaby. When we were working on *Lady and the Tramp,* I remember him saying once, "Hey, what the hell's wrong with a lullaby? You guys are just too hardened. You don't feel things anymore."

jim algar DIRECTOR

When you worked around Walt, everything was yes answers or hopeful answers. He never, for a minute, entertained the no answers. He didn't suffer people who were cynics or skeptics because they got in his way.

roy o. disney BROTHER

When the banks were closed in 1933, of course I was frantic—What are we gonna do for money? So I was stewing and worrying and Walt was impatient with me. He said, "Quit worrying about it. People aren't going to stop living just because the banks are closed. What the hell, we'll make potatoes the medium of exchange. We'll pay everybody in potatoes!"

buddy baker COMPOSER

Animator Woolie Reitherman used to wear red shirts and I had a red sports shirt too. Walt hated our red shirts. Every time I would see him when I had that red shirt on, he would say, "Hmmph. I suppose that shirt makes you feel younger…"

One day, I passed Woolie in the hall and he had his red shirt on and I had my red shirt on, and he asked, "Have you seen Walt today?"

"No," I answered.

"Don't!" he warned.

bob gurr IMAGINEER

When Don Burnham, the chairman of Westinghouse, got close to Walt, his bottom lip would start quivering and it was hard for him to speak. When some people got too close to Walt, they got spooked because they idolized Walt Disney.

Walt was aware of this and he would deliberately dress down by undoing a button or slopping up his tie so it was askew. He tried to send a signal, "I'm okay."

I remember one meeting where he showed up wearing a ratty-looking trench coat with a little porkpie hat that he kept crumpled up in the coat pocket. He was like Peter Falk as Columbo on television. Everything was a bit askew so people would know he was regular. He knew he scared the daylights out of people and didn't want to let that get in the way of being able to work with them. Otherwise all he'd have is a bunch of people agreeing with him and their expertise wouldn't show.

ben sharpsteen DIRECTOR

At the Studio, we were always eager to keep pace with Walt—what he was trying to achieve and how he was thinking. We used to say that Walt was a hound dog. He was hot on a trail and we would follow him, but as he led us, we would lose him. He was far ahead of us. We would plunge on blindly and find ourselves hanging onto the old trail or as we put it, the end of a trend. Walt had deviated from the trail and found an even hotter scent and a much better one too.

THE "WOUNDED BEAR": HIS MOODS AND TEMPERAMENT

tommie wilck WALT'S SECRETARY

During the first year I was up in his office, there were times when he wore what we called his "wounded bear suit," when he was just meaner than poison. This particular time, he'd been wearing his wounded bear suit for several days and I was, frankly, getting a little fed up with it. He had called me on something I had already told him about earlier in the day.

I said something like, "As I told you this morning…"

And he said, "You don't need to be so damned sassy about it!" He was furious. With that he got up from his desk, walked to the door, turned around and said, "You don't have to work here. There are other places where you can go."

I took that to mean he fired me. By this time I was crying, I was so mad. So I gathered up all the stuff from my desk. When he came back, he went to his desk and called me to come in. He never said he was sorry. He just said I didn't need to look for another job and added, "But, you *were* sassy!"

buddy baker COMPOSER

As we would come through the front gate of the Studio, we'd get a signal from the guard about Walt's mood. If he looked like he was in a bad mood that morning, the guard would warn, "bear suit."

ollie johnston ANIMATOR

If Walt was irritated about something, he'd say, "Hello, Oliver." Whereas, if everything was fine, he'd say, "Hi, Ollie!" He did the same with Frank Thomas, he'd say, "Hello, Franklin."

frank thomas ANIMATOR

There was this drumming of the fingers on the arm of the chair and that was when he'd just stare at you for as long as ten minutes or more. Usually, he wasn't thinking about you at all; you just happened to be in his line of vision, although you never knew for sure.

harrison "buzz" price
RESEARCH CONSULTANT

He treated me with paternal affection; however, he chewed me out a couple of times. One of those times, I was on his airplane serving highballs. Walt looked at me with his eyebrow up and said, "You're too fat to fly on my airplane!" I was 210 pounds, which was heavy for me. He was on a tear that night. He started ripping on Donn Tatum for about two hours. He was telling Donn, "Don't get between me and my brother. I don't need you to interpret my relationship with my brother."

At midnight that night, we got to the hotel and Walt said, "What I said to you on the plane—I meant it." So I lost 36 pounds within 13 weeks. When I was a lean 170 pounds, he said, "Buzz, you're getting positively handsome."

roy e. disney NEPHEW

I was working on this little TV show called *The Legend of El Blanco*. It had a song in it that Paul Smith and Hazel George had written. I didn't play the song for Walt first, which I should have done. So as I was showing him the footage I had put together, about halfway through, he said, "I don't like the song, Roy." The song kept cropping up all the way through and every time, he said, "I don't like this song." Finally, the lights went on and he was like, "I *really* don't like this song, Roy."

I didn't know what to say, so I replied, "I kinda like it, Walt." Wrong! He turned on me like a snake striking and said, "Do you want to work on this thing or not?" His eyebrow went clear to the top of his forehead.

"Yeah, sure," I said—in terror!

"Okay," he said, "then let's fix it." We actually had a lot of fun making the show after that, but man, it was tough.

ward kimball ANIMATOR

We got on the train and had staterooms right next to each other and off we went to the Chicago Railroad Fair. About the second day out, he said, "I can't understand some of the guys…" and he named names. "They seem to have a lot of talent, but they don't say anything at meetings."

He tried to get me to tell him why. Finally, I said, "You scare 'em. Lots of times you jump on them because their ideas don't fit yours. Everything they do, you throw out."

"Well, sometimes by doing it wrong," he said, "it shows me the right way."

roy e. disney NEPHEW

When someone came back from a meeting we'd say,
"How'd it go?" The answer might be, "He had his
'wounded bear' suit on, but he didn't have it zipped up,"
meaning it was awful, but I survived it. If the bear suit was
zipped, that was really bad.

$\mathscr{A}$TTITUDES AND PHILOSOPHIES

peter ellenshaw ARTIST

Walt would say, "We're making corn, Peter. I know it's not your kind of corn, but it's got to be *good* corn. Let's make it the best we possibly can. We're trying to please people."

roy williams ANIMATOR

He said, "When you're making pictures for an audience, you never play over their heads and you never play underneath them. You play straight out at them." In other words, don't get highbrow by going over their heads and don't insult their intelligence by doing something too corny. You play right straight at the American people and they love you and understand everything.

ollie johnston ANIMATOR

Walt said, "You don't worry about logic, you put entertainment ahead of logic."

frank thomas ANIMATOR

Walt never wanted to do the same thing twice. He said, "I don't want just a picture. It's got to be a new experience, a new theatrical experience."

roy e. disney NEPHEW

His notion was that money was there, to make things with, that would make money, which was different from Dad's attitude, which was if you don't have the money, you can't make the thing in the first place.

Walt's attitude about it, which was very astute, was "If I make something that people want to see, we're going to do fine." So his business sense was centered on creating, while Dad was sort of the flip side of that, which was one reason why the partnership worked so well.

roy o. disney BROTHER

We were never at odds about money. Walt just wanted more of it. We needed more of it, that's all. He spent it faster than I could get it back sometimes.

william "joe" potter
THEME PARK EXECUTIVE

Once, when I tried to explain to Walt that something was going to cost a million dollars, he said, "When are you going to learn not to bother me with inconsequential details?"

eric larson ANIMATOR

His effort was toward perfection. Perfection was something you kept your eye on, something you strove for, and once in a while attained.

bill martin IMAGINEER

Walt used to say, "I don't care what you can't do. I want to hear what you *can* do." If there were fifteen ways to solve a problem, Walt was looking for all fifteen.

hayley mills ACTRESS

Looking back, I appreciate even more now what Walt was trying to do with his movies. He told me that he wanted to show people the best in themselves. Certainly, he achieved that. You always come out of his movies feeling happier than when you went in and you feel better about humanity and the human condition.

john hench ARTIST

When Walt built Disneyland, he was trying to make people feel better about themselves. I think he had discovered what people were looking for—the feeling of being alive and in love with life.

He integrated the same philosophy when he created the environment of Disneyland. He arranged those forms and colors in ways to evoke emotion. He understood people enough to know that you don't give them problems to think about, but something to feel good about.

van arsdale france DISNEYLAND EXECUTIVE

One time at Disneyland, Walt saw something in the trash and said to a staff member, "Take care of that trash."

The guy responded, "I'll call the custodial department." That was the wrong thing to say. Anybody who would say, "That's not my job," Walt gladly got rid of.

john culhane JOURNALIST

When I was seventeen, through the good offices of Walt Disney's daughter, Diane, I met Walt—as he insisted I call him. We strolled and conversed in the backyard of his Holmby Hills home. The subject was happiness, which Walt defined as "spontaneous delight harmonized with circum-stances." He summed up his philosophy of happiness by starting to sing to me a song from the 1925 Broadway musical *No, No, Nanette.* Walt warbled, "I want to be happy, but I won't be happy 'til I make you happy too. Life's really worth living when we are mirth-giving. Why can't I give some to you?" I chimed in too.

Walt never mentioned to me that day about his latest dream—Disneyland. But he did tell me that "Life should be a World's Fair of delights."

"I know that life isn't…" he said. "But I think it should be, I believe it could be and hope it will be."

john hench ARTIST

I was questioning Walt about using real leather and wood in the Disneyland stagecoaches. I thought people wouldn't appreciate the elegant work. "Now, wait a minute," he said. "People will respect what you do because you have done it so well." Then he tapped me on the chest with his big, bony finger and explained that misunderstanding is a result of information that's either wrong or late. He said, "People act with good intentions. People are *really* okay!" He believed that.

roy o. disney BROTHER

Walt looked at bookkeepers and lawyers and bankers as the cement you had to put in the foundation of a building. Necessary—yes, but you couldn't see it and you couldn't peddle it. It was part of the drag of doing business.

diane disney miller DAUGHTER

Dad used to say, "Now that you're up, there's no place you can go but down. But when you're down, you can always go up."

winston hibler PRODUCER

Walt always said, "I'm a happy ending guy."

ARTIST, STORYTELLER AND ANIMATION PIONEER

lillian disney WIFE

In the early days, after we had dinner, Walt used to drive around to catch the cartoons at the theaters. He knew what time they were playing and would drive to each theater and leave me in the car with the dog and my mother while he saw the cartoons. He studied them all—*Felix the Cat, Out of the Inkwell*—to learn from them.

There wasn't a night we didn't end up at the Studio. We'd go out for a ride someplace and inevitably he'd say, "I've got just one little thing I want to do." I slept on the davenport while he worked. Sometimes I'd wake up and say, "How late is it?"

"Oh, it's not late," he'd say, even though it was three in the morning.

ken anderson ARTIST

Walt gave us all a 65-cent dinner, which was a sumptuous meal at the time, and then went through the whole *Snow White* story for us. From beginning to end, he performed the characters and their voices and we all fell for the story. We sat from eight until nearly midnight, spellbound. He took this simple story and embroidered it.

joe grant STORY ARTIST

Walt would go from room to room and tell that whole damn *Snow White* story until we were bored stiff. And at each stop, he picked up something new from somebody's reaction. The story was never written; there was never a script; it was in his mind.

marc davis ANIMATOR

People cried when Snow White died and the dwarfs took off their little hats and tears rolled down their faces. People wiped their eyes over these drawings as they appeared on the screen. This is one of the most remarkable things that Walt created. This was the thing that he searched for: to make you believe they were real.

roy e. disney NEPHEW

Walt realized pretty early on that if there isn't an emotional weight to *Snow White*, it's not going to work. Everything that was done in that movie was about making sure you care about the characters.

shirley temple black ACTRESS

In 1939, when I saw the specially designed Oscar I was to present to Walt for *Snow White and the Seven Dwarfs*, I knew the big one was for Walt and the seven little ones standing in a row were for the dwarfs and I asked, "Where's Snow White's award?" Walt chuckled; he had a twinkle in his eye.

john hench   ARTIST

We were in a famous Detroit restaurant and Walt was in a good mood. He drew a sketch of me on the napkin. It was kind of a cartoon, very freely done, and he said, "People think I can't draw. But I can draw."

diane disney miller   DAUGHTER

Dad's autograph was a work of art. He would begin to wind up his hand before it even hit the paper.

ben sharpsteen   DIRECTOR

In the early days, when we were making animated shorts, Walt was driving through town and was stopped by a cop, who gave him a ticket. He returned to the Studio and told us about it. He reenacted his conversation with the cop in a way that revealed he did not think it was very funny. Each time he told the story, however, it became funnier and his attitude changed. And before we knew it, we were starting a picture called *Traffic Troubles*.

john hench ARTIST

When you told a story to Walt, you had to stand in front of the board with a pointer and explain the action of each drawing. You had to keep your eye on him because he'd drift off at any minute. And if you turned your back on him, you'd never know at what point you'd lost him.

Walt would go into kind of a trance. In his mind, he could see the whole story so well and bend forward unconsciously and become like an old owl—hunched up, and his bill would clack a little bit. When he'd come out of it, he'd say, "You know what we ought to do is..." and then he'd leap up and begin acting out the scene with all-new dialogue and business.

winston hibler PRODUCER

Harry Reeves and Homer Brighton had presented their storyboard to Walt and he had cut it up pretty good; he didn't like it at all. When Walt left the room and started down the hall, Harry took a kick at the storyboard and drove his foot through it. He had his foot in the board up to his ankle when Walt came back into the room with another idea. Nothing was said. Walt knew exactly what had happened and he just busted up laughing, turned around and walked back down the hall.

roy e. disney NEPHEW

I was getting over the chicken pox. This was probably 1938 or '39, not long after *Snow White*. Walt and Lilly came over for dinner and he came up to my room just to say, "Hi." He sat down on the edge of my bed and said, "You know, we're working on this new story and I want to tell you about it." He told me the whole story of *Pinocchio*. I'll bet he was there for thirty minutes acting out all the parts, like he usually did. Then when the picture came out, it was a huge letdown to me...nowhere near as good as his personal version of it.

lisa davis VOICE OF ANITA

To prepare me as the voice of Anita in *101 Dalmatians*, Walt had me sit in a bungalow at the Studio with a litter of Dalmatian puppies every single day. He and I would sit and play with the puppies together. It was delightful.

He said, "Do you know what they're like now? Do you understand the Dalmatian?"

"Yes, yes, I do!"

frank thomas ANIMATOR

Down in Argentina, they had a competition among children, and those who won had this special prize of watching Walt Disney draw up on the stage of a big theater. So he got together with me and Fergie [Norman Ferguson] the night before and said, "Hey, you guys have to teach me how to draw some of these characters."

We tried to explain Mickey to him and then Goofy. So finally, we said, "Why don't we put the drawing in blue pencil for you because the footlights on stage will reflect on the paper and knock out the blue so the audience won't see it."

He watched us to see what we drew first and what we drew second and on down the line, trying to get the feel of it. Then he said, "If you guys see I'm doing something wrong, you come over and I'll make some kind of gag out of it."

What we didn't know was that the twelve kids would come up on the stage and stand right beside Walt as he drew. From that vantage point the blue lines were very clear and Walt tried to cover them with his body, looking more and more like a frantic spider than a confident artist. Since no one on the stage spoke English besides the three of us, he could express his feelings out loud about the "two dirty guys who talked me into this," "stop laughing," and "whose idea was it to draw this in blue first, anyway?"

chuck jones ANIMATION PRODUCER

Walt is the patron saint of animation. He made us all possible. At Warner Bros., we thought Disney Studios was creating Rolls-Royces and we were making Model T Fords. But we were satisfied with our Model T Fords.

The thing that Walt understood was that the animator counts. Movement is what makes our method of communication different from any other art form. It's more than just beautiful drawings and Walt understood that.

roy williams ANIMATOR

We'd do gags and then we wouldn't like them ourselves, so we would wrinkle them up and throw them in the wastebasket. Now Walt would come in at night, after we all went home and go through those wastebaskets. The janitor had orders not to touch anything in the room until he went through it. The next morning, we'd come into work and there'd be a bunch of wadded drawings, straightened out, pinned up on the storyboard with Walt's note saying, "Use this. It's a good gag."

frank thomas ANIMATOR

Day after day, Walt listened to the music for *Fantasia* and talked about it and his reaction was, "Gee, I can remember going to concerts as a kid—the orchestra coming out onto the stage, tuning up and then they'd start playing. All the fiddles would come up at the same time."

He was reacting emotionally to the visual experience as part of a total experience and his whole concept of *Fantasia* was that way. He didn't care so much about the highbrow, the background, the esoteric, what the music is supposed to mean, or how it was supposed to be, or what had been said over the years. It was all a part of a farm boy in Kansas. How do I react to this music? Do I see images? Does it make me feel like this or this? It was all feeling.

roy o. disney BROTHER

Walt, Leopold Stokowski and Deems Taylor were talking over *Fantasia*. They were playing records and discussing the various musical numbers. I joined this session and during the course of it dared to say, "My Gosh! Can't you select music that just an ordinary guy like me can like?" They all froze and Walt ordered me out of the room—"Go back and keep the books!"

ben sharpsteen DIRECTOR

A sequence in *Bambi* had grown far too long. In desperation, Walt sat in the projection room with the directing animator to cut the sequence down. Walt would say, "You can cut here" or "Cut this scene out entirely." The director complained, "I think I would lose something if we cut that out."

Walt was exasperated. He stopped short and said, "Here I am, losing my shirt, and you're telling me what *you'd* be losing."

ilene woods VOICE OF CINDERELLA

We had finished recording "Sing Sweet Nightingale" and Walt came in at the end of the day. He'd always listen to our recordings with his head down, resting in his hands. This particular time he looked up at me and asked, "Ilene, can you sing harmony with yourself? I envision Cinderella scrubbing the floor and a soap bubble rise and I hear a second-part harmony begin. Then I see another soap bubble rise and hear a third-part harmony kick in and so on and so on until we've got about an eight-part harmony going."

So he had me sing the song and then record the second-part harmony and so on. They mixed all the parts together and it was such a beautiful animation sequence because each time the bubble would rise, so would another voice and it blended so well because it was all the same voice. When I heard the finished product, Walt said, "How about that? All of these years I've been paying three salaries for the Andrews Sisters, when I could have paid only one for you!"

joe grant STORY ARTIST

He could feel the music. In *Fantasia*, there's a lot of his soul in that picture.

ward kimball ANIMATOR

Walt was a great admirer of Chaplin. He was always showing us how Chaplin did a certain gag. We thought Walt was just as good a pantomimist as Chaplin. Of course, if you asked Walt to do any acting, he'd get a little self-conscious, but when he would get carried away with a story or gag situation and start imitating something, he was just as great as Chaplin.

frank thomas ANIMATOR

Walt was so funny when he played the voice of Mickey Mouse in *The Pointer*. Every time he'd go through the scene between the bear and Mickey, we all got to laughing. He'd say, "I'm Mickey Mouse, you know? Mickey Mouse? You've heard of me…I hope. I hope." At one point Dave Hand said, "Wouldn't it be great if we got a camera on Walt for this?" Walt was reticent, however, because he hadn't done any work in front of the camera. He didn't feel like he wanted to act, but he couldn't say the lines without acting. So he finally said, "If you're filming from the control booth and I can't see what you're doing and it's just me and the microphone, then okay."

ollie johnston ANIMATOR

Walt acted out the movements of Baloo the Bear in the hall after a meeting. He invented the little step I had Baloo do, which was the key to the bear's personality.

lillian disney WIFE

Walt always acted out scenes—to the sky, the birds, to anything. He was always making gestures while talking. I remember once in Palm Springs he was out on the terrace, completely engrossed in what he was doing—laughing and acting out something he was working on. He was never embarrassed if someone saw him.

frank thomas ANIMATOR

We always felt he never really knew how we animated and he resented this to a certain extent. He'd tease us and needle us about "I'm going to find a way to replace you guys. If I get these Audio-Animatronics figures working, the first thing I'm going to do is teach them to animate!" He knew the mechanics of animation, but what process we went through to take a story idea and create a character, a drawing with life and personality—I don't think he really could grasp it.

richard sherman SONGWRITER

The end scene of *The Jungle Book*, when this pretty girl sings and flirts with Mowgli and he shrugs and goes off with her—that was the Disney touch. He put that little piece of heart in there. For the most part, the film was fun, slam-bam and socko stuff. But, like Chaplin, Walt had that secret of always putting in a little tear someplace.

lillian disney WIFE

He was wonderful at sketching. He had a crude style but there was always lots of action. He never became a good artist because he directed. He was so much more a director than an artist.

FORT DISNEY: THE STRIKE AND WAR YEARS

ollie johnston ANIMATOR

During the war, I'd run into Walt on the lot. He'd lean against the wall and just stand there not talking very much. I'd try to carry on a conversation but it was very difficult because he seemed so depressed. One time I asked him, "How do you think *Ichabod and Mr. Toad* will do?"

He said, "It'll do all right, but we gotta get this place so it doesn't hang on one picture all the time. I gotta get the unions and stockholders and bankers off my back."

joe grant STORY ARTIST

Before the strike, Walt thought socialism was about
everybody pulling together. He was an extreme liberal at
one time. He even considered putting apartments on the
Studio lot for his employees, so we'd all live there as one
big, happy family.

ollie johnston ANIMATOR

I can remember about the second day of the strike; we'd
just come through the line and Walt was standing there
with his hat on at a funny angle and his coat over his arm,
kind of smiling at the guys on the line. He hollered
something to one of them in a friendly way and said, "Aw,
they'll be back in a couple of days." He didn't really realize
the true situation, that some of them were real bitter.

marc davis ANIMATOR

A lot of us were kind of pulled into the union as prestige members whenever there was a problem or something. I was up in Walt's office and mentioned something about this to Walt and I said, "You ought to meet the union's business agent. He's a nice guy."

"Look Marc," Walt said, "if I met him, I probably would like him very much." And then he told me about the early days in New York and Pat Powers, who just stole him blind.

He said, "I just loved Pat and he did these awful things to me. Marc, I don't want to meet this man, I might like him."

joe grant STORY ARTIST

The strike caused resentment and he was a changed man after that. I think he was a fair man; he would have done most of the stuff they were fighting for, but they didn't give him a chance and that burned him up. As Walt recuperated, he built Disneyland.

ken anderson ARTIST

We had a bunch of storyboards to present to Walt, which I was supposed to do. Walt sat to my left and to his left was Alexander Seversky, the czar's ace, who wrote *Victory Through Air Power*. A bunch of army and navy brass were sitting all around. It just so happened to be my birthday and I had been given a new cigarette lighter. I had overfilled it that morning without knowing it and hadn't used it yet.

Walt took a cigarette out and put it in his mouth. I took the cue and got my lighter out. I lit the thing and it was a bonfire! It burned his mustache and the end of his nose. He jumped clean out of his chair, holding his face and said, "What the hell are you trying to do?" and he went flying out of the room.

Then all these people filed out of the room and I was sitting there alone. I could have died. In fact, dying would have been a pleasure compared to the way I felt.

Word got around the Studio. All that day, I was ignored by my friends. Nobody would even walk near me. If they

saw me coming, they'd duck into a hall, out of the way. I was a skunk. I actually cried that night, I felt so badly.

I came in the next morning and people were still avoiding me like the plague. I sat at my desk; I just didn't know what the hell to do and the phone rang. It was Walt. He said, "Hi, Ken. What are you doing for lunch?" I said, "Nothing, I guess."

"I'll meet you," he said. "I've got some things I want to talk to you about. I'll pick you up at your office." I wondered if he was firing me, because he sounded so jovial.

He had shaved his mustache clear off and he had this blister on the end of his nose. I knew better than to say a damn thing about it. He took me to lunch. We walked through the line in the cafeteria and he sat at the table with me and conversed all the way through lunch. Walt never even mentioned the incident at all. He wanted everybody at the Studio to see I wasn't out on a limb. It took a pretty wonderful humanitarian to do what he did.

t. hee DIRECTOR

Major Seversky had one leg. It had been shot off in World War I and he wore a false leg that had a habit of squeaking as he walked from one part of the set to another while they were filming scenes. We had a sound man at that time, named Sam, who had an ear just like an owl. He could hear everything and would say, "There's a squeak in the background."

So they shot the scene again and Sam heard this squeak about three times and Walt said, "What the hell's the squeak, Sam?"

Seversky said, "I think it must be my leg" and he swung it back and forth and added, "It's squeaky."

Walt said, "Oh, hell, my knee squeaks like that sometimes. Leave the squeak in, Sam."

jim fletcher ARTIST

During the war years, the Studio had car sharing. On Walt's day, he'd go around and pick up artists and secretaries and bring them to the Studio.

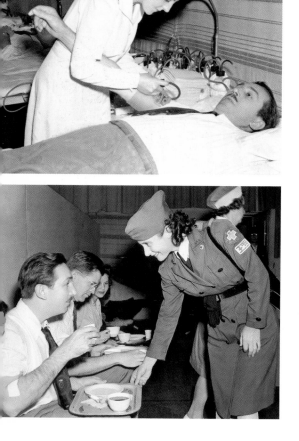

charlie ridgway THEME PARK PUBLICIST

Cyril James, who worked for the Disney London office, told me that despite the fact that the Studio was losing money during the war, without fail they received a care package from Walt and Roy every week. And many times that was virtually the only food they had each week throughout the war.

ken anderson ARTIST

The challenge for Walt was to try to do something that was practical for the war effort and still try to get in a little entertainment. Walt was strong on that. He didn't like to produce commercials or documentaries. Things had to be entertaining.

LIVE-ACTION FILM PRODUCER

frank thomas ANIMATOR

Walt used to kid us about "Those actors out there—boy, you give 'em the lines and they rehearse it a couple of times and you're done! You guys (animators) take six months for a line!" He had a twinkle in his eye, but he was mainly serious.

bill anderson PRODUCER

Even before *Song of the South* was complete, Walt was ready to do live-action stories. He talked to me about it. He said, "We won't turn into a live-action studio, but we'll get into this live-action business."

bill walsh PRODUCER

Walt always said, "Try and learn what the hell we're doing. Go to the theater where your film is playing. Listen to the way the audience responds to it. It should sound like Moses comin' down from the mountain with the commandments."

dick van dyke ACTOR

Once I read the *Mary Poppins* script, I saw the part of the old banker, and thought, "Oh, I'd love to be that character too." So I asked Walt about it. I said, "This won't cost you another nickel; I won't charge you any more for the two parts. I just want to do it."

Walt was really an old horse trader. I not only had to do a screen test for the role, but I had to donate $4,000 to Walt's then new art school—CalArts! You didn't get anything for nothing from old Walt.

karen dotrice ACTRESS

I clearly remember being in Walt's office one time and, from a child's point of view, it was a great long walk from the door over to this enormous desk located at the far side of the room. I remember saying, "Uncle Walt, why don't you move your desk closer to the door?"

"Oh, darlin'," he said. "I have to tell you why. It's not a very nice thing, but it's a little bit of human psychology that we use in this business."

"What are you talking about?" I asked.

"By the time the fat, wedgy, gargantuan executives have crossed the floor," he explained, "they lose their courage to ask me for what they originally came in for."

diane disney miller DAUGHTER

At home, we'd see dailies with very sentimental scenes from films like *Song of the South* or *So Dear to My Heart*. I didn't like it; I'd squirm in my seat and criticize the scenes, which infuriated Dad. After a while, he stopped bringing the dailies home.

glynis johns ACTRESS

I got a call one day to have lunch with Walt to talk about *Mary Poppins*. I had been performing on stage in New York and had just finished the pilot for my own series, *The Glynis Show*. As we were having lunch, I said, "I'll tell you one thing, I think I'm going to get very depressed if everybody else around me is singing and I'm not. With my own series coming up now and having just finished a play on Broadway, I'm a little tired so I would need a musical incentive to see me through the project. Music lifts me up."

After our meeting, I drove to the Chateau Marmont on the Sunset Strip, where I was staying. It took about forty minutes to arrive there from the Studio. As I was coming through the door of my apartment, the telephone was ringing; it was Walt! He said, "Hold on a minute." During that short time, he had the Sherman Brothers write a song for me and they began singing the chorus of "Sister Suffragette" over the phone. I had no more doubts.

dean jones ACTOR

Walt would come to the set of *That Darn Cat* very often with the attitude of a tourist from Duluth, rather than the authority figure at the Studio, asking the pet trainer questions like, "How did you train the cat to jump up on the ironing board, walk to the end, and jump up and get the duck hanging from the rafters?"

126

patty disney NIECE

When Walt ran *Pollyanna*, I wept out loud through the entire movie and he said, "Great! Just go ahead and cry!" My reaction to his movie pleased him thoroughly.

roy e. disney NEPHEW

When I was working on *The Vanishing Prairie*, Jim Algar, the producer, had put together sort of an outline on film of what we had so far. It began with spring on the prairie and the thaw and the northward migration of geese and ducks. We had a couple of shots of some ducks coming in for a landing on a pond that was still frozen. There was a shot of one particular duck, who came in and landed and didn't realize it was ice. He started to go ass-over-teakettle and the cameraman apparently didn't like the shot and cut the camera.

So anyway, we ran the show with that shot cut in—in its entirety—and Walt asked, "Where's the rest of the shot where the duck slides into the other ducks?"

Lloyd Richardson, the editor, replied, "Well, we don't have that, Walt."

"Oh, yes, you do," he insisted. "I saw it." So we get back to the office and Lloyd turned to me and said, "Go find it."

Over the next three or four months, I looked through every bit of film footage we owned and it wasn't there. Then every time we'd run it, Walt would say, "Where's the rest of that stuff? It's there somewhere!" So I'd have to go back and look again.

Finally, Jim sent a cameraman up to Minnesota and he found a pond that had frozen over and he got a bunch of ducks. If you looked closely, you could see they were tame ducks. Somebody off camera was sliding this duck into the group…over and over.

So we took the best of the footage and cut it in and needless to say, added the sound of bowling balls and Walt said, "I told you, you had this stuff!"

127

kurt russell ACTOR

Some of the things Walt and I laughed about were if you could create movies in a way so people think they're looking through a window and seeing something they aren't necessarily supposed to see. If you could create that kind of a feeling with an audience, then you've done your job. We used to talk about ways we could create that illusion. It was kind of an impish thing between us. I always felt he was chuckling in his mind.

ken annakin DIRECTOR

You had to be careful in a story conference that you did not dismiss an idea from the top of Walt's head as impractical. If you did, it would inevitably find its place in your movie.

On *Swiss Family Robinson*, Walt came up with the idea of Kevin Corcoran making friends with a tiger. I said, "Walt, I worked with two supposedly tame lions in South Africa and they were difficult...very time consuming."

He picked up on this and said to the producer and writer, "Obviously, Ken's afraid of working with a tiger." At every meeting thereafter he would bring up some great tiger incident and then say, "But we can't do that because Ken is afraid of tigers." Of course, the tiger stayed in the film and played a very important role.

vernon scott JOURNALIST

I've always thought that of all the successful producers and studio heads, Walt was the most interesting. Harry Cohn, Louis B. Mayer, Jack Warner, or even Zanuck, who was maybe the next best producer, weren't creative men like Disney was.

He was a creative artist who was forced to become a businessman. Those other guys were businessmen who invaded the arts. That's what set Walt apart. He was always on the side of quality and art, not just the buck. He liked the almighty dollar as well as the next man, but he wanted to put quality up on the screen.

128

richard sherman SONGWRITER

A critic had written a snide article in some high-profile news magazine about *The Absent-Minded Professor*. Other critics had also taken it the wrong way. Walt just couldn't understand the response to this film. *The Absent-Minded Professor* was such a funny idea.

Walt sucked on his tooth, which he always did, looked out his office window at the Studio and said, "You know, I've got all those mouths to feed… Well, I still think the majority of people are gonna like that picture."

Don't let anybody ever tell you Walt was immune to a bad review. It bothered him! The good reviews never went to his head, but the bad reviews went to his heart.

ken anderson ARTIST

He was always planning new worlds to conquer. He was certainly way ahead of his time with everything—color, sound, you name it. I can remember *Song of the South*, which was his first color combination of live action and animation. He had me doing all these things before the sodium vapor screen was ever created. We did rear projection. We tried everything. I was too stupid to realize that he was using everything as an experiment. I kept thinking he wanted problems solved. Then when I'd get something solved, he'd want to do something different. I thought, "What the hell does he want to do it differently for?" because I'd worked like hell to get this thing to work and now he wanted to change everything. I didn't realize he wasn't capable of saying why he wanted to change things. He just wanted to find better and newer ways of doing everything.

diane disney miller DAUGHTER

After he saw the movie *To Kill a Mockingbird*, he said, "I wish I could make a movie like that." I think he wanted to do something meaningful, a little more adult.

winston hibler PRODUCER

We had a technical adviser on *The Absent-Minded Professor* and after a while, Walt half-seriously thought it might be possible to actually develop something like Flubber. In other words, to Walt, there had to be credibility. The audience had to be able to say, "Yes, even in a wild, crazy way that could be true."

george bruns COMPOSER

He thought of music as a supporting actor. It supports the picture. He liked music to come in on a dissolve and carry over into the next scene. He used to say over and over again, "Music's got to carry the story from one scene to another."

richard fleischer DIRECTOR

I must have worked as a director at RKO for six or seven years when my agent called and said, "Walt Disney says he'd like you to meet with him at the Studio."

I was curious, since he and my father, Max Fleischer, had been long-time competitors. Walt was constantly luring away my father's animators. It felt funny to walk through Disney Studios, which was considered an enemy camp in my home.

I met Walt in his office and he asked, "Do you recognize this picture on the wall?" He had a vivid painting of a submarine entangled with a giant squid. Its title was "20,000 Leagues Under the Sea." "We're going to make it into a movie," he said.

"That sounds great," I said. "In animation, of course."

"No! It will be a live-action film," he said. "I want you to direct it."

I nearly fainted when he said that. "You know who I am, don't you?" I asked.

He laughed and said, "Yes, I know. Do you want to do this picture?"

"More than anything I want to do this picture," I said. "But I can't accept it immediately because of my father. I wouldn't want him to feel I was being disloyal to him by working for you."

"I understand," he said "Why don't you phone your father tonight and then call me tomorrow morning."

So as soon as I got home, I called my father and explained the situation to him and he said, "You really *must* take this picture. You absolutely have my blessing. Now, give Walt a message for me: Tell him I say he's got great taste in directors."

The tag to this story is that, later, Walt called and said, "I'd like to have your dad over to the Studio for a luncheon and I'll invite all his ex-employees." Then he gave my father a special VIP tour of Disneyland and they ended up becoming friends.

lew hunter SCREENWRITER

We were talking once while he was filming *Old Yeller*, and he said to me, "It's really quite a thing." Now, he would never say it's quite a responsibility. He said, "It's really quite a thing being where I am. Killing Bambi's mother was a tough thing for me. We had talked about it back and forth and finally decided that was the way to go. Then I showed it to the employees before we released it, and my daughter Diane was there. I put her in bed after the screening and she was crying. 'Honey,' I said, 'what's the matter?'

"'Bambi's mother died.' I said, 'Oh, honey. It was just a movie.' She accentuated her weeping and said, 'But Daddy, you could have made Bambi's mother live!'" The heaviest thing on Walt's mind at that time was trying to decide whether Old Yeller should live or die.

dean jones ACTOR

I had an interesting lunch with Walt once. There were five things that I felt were kind of corny and old-fashioned in *Blackbeard's Ghost,* which I thought should be taken out. On two of them, Walt said, "Okay, but you're pushing your luck." On the fourth and fifth point he got upset and said, "If there are so many things about this picture you don't like, you don't have to do it. I'll get another actor!"

"Look, Walt," I said. "I'm not asking for more closeups. I'm not asking for more money. I'm trying to make the picture better and I'm just pointing out that we've seen this joke one hundred times on screen and I don't think it's funny anymore."

Walt countered, "That joke was funny in 1923 and it'll be funny today!" (The joke stayed in the picture and I laughed at it along with the rest of the audience at the premiere. Walt was right!)

On another one of my objections, Walt dug in his heels. Later, we were walking back toward his office and he started up the steps of the Animation Building. We said goodbye and I was walking on when he stopped me. "Oh, that scene with the phony gun—we'll do it *your* way." Then he pointed his finger at me and added, "but you better be right!" And I knew I'd better be.

richard sherman SONGWRITER

Walt pulled a book off his shelf and said, "My daughters and wife think this is very good. I read it and think there's a lot in it. Read this and tell me what you think," and he handed us this book, *Mary Poppins*.

Bob and I read it twice over a weekend. There was no story line, only a series of incidents. We invented a kind of story from six of its chapters. Then we called his secretary and asked, "Can we please have an hour with Walt?"

At the meeting, we started telling Walt our version of the story and singing song ideas we had developed. He let us free-flow. Walt said, "Let me see your notes." When we showed him our copy of the book, he looked at the table of contents, which we had marked up and said, "Ha, ha!" Then he took his book off the shelf and showed it to us. He had underlined the exact same six chapters!

buddy baker COMPOSER

I remember sitting in one of those sweatboxes with George Bruns and Walt when a couple of other people came in. George whispered to me, "I've got a door slam down here that's outa sync by two frames. Let's see if it gets by him."

So the door slam played and about five minutes later, Walt turned around and said, "George, you're about two frames late on that door slam."

bill walsh PRODUCER

He had an instinct—the instinct that made Disney, Disney. He sensed things in Julie Andrews even though she had never done a picture. We did a make-up test and it was only on the screen three seconds when Walt said, "We're home!" She had a stunning empathy. Only Walt—and the camera—knew it instantly.

bill walsh PRODUCER

He said, "When you want to discover kids with star quality, just watch them at recess. You will always find one kid you can't help but watch." How Walt knew things like that, I don't know. He knew things no one else knew in this town.

The only story Walt ever wrote was *Lt. Robin Crusoe, U.S.N.* He wrote it on the back of an envelope or throw-up bag on the airplane. I said, "Walt, you don't want your name on this, do you?"

"I do, too!" he said. And he did. His name appears backwards in the credits—Retlaw Yensid.

richard sherman SONGWRITER

After we won our two Academy Awards for the music of *Mary Poppins*, we came to the Studio real early the next morning and put our Oscars on Walt's desk, and asked his secretary to call us when he came in.

He was sitting behind his desk and our four Oscars were shining in his face. He acted as though he didn't even see them. When we walked in he said, "Well, boys, you hit one out of the park, but remember the bases were loaded."

CHANNELING WALT:
TV'S MOST COLORFUL CELEBRITY

herb ryman ARTIST

Walt's daughter Diane and her husband, Ron, were
sitting in the den. We were having a conversation and Ron
turned on the TV to watch a football game. I'd look over
every once in a while at the game. Then Walt got up, walked
over to the TV and said to Ron, "Do you mind if I turn this
thing off," and he turned it off, "Television is antisocial." Walt
wanted everybody to be a part of the conversation.

Then Lilly said, "He says TV is antisocial, but wait until
his program comes out in the fall! He'll want everybody to
look at the TV then!"

lillian disney WIFE

When the children weren't home, we ate alone and almost always in front of the television. He looked at everything; we'd get a lousy program and I'd say, "Do you want me to change it?"

"No, no. I just want to study it," he'd say. I'd get annoyed and go upstairs and let him keep watching it. He was the same with pictures. I'd say, "That one had a bad review."

"I don't care," he'd say. "I want to see what the director did."

bill walsh PRODUCER

Walt was terrified when we were going on television. I said, "Walt, they gotta have you on." Once he began performing every week, however, he kinda liked it. It uncovered a streak of ham in him.

kathryn beaumont VOICE OF ALICE

During the filming of the "One Hour in Wonderland" television broadcast, which was Walt's first television special, he was performing in scenes with us. He was a little uncomfortable about his role because he wanted to do it right. He was concerned about remembering his lines.

bobby burgess MOUSEKETEER

So many of the producers thought Jimmie Dodd was the perfect guy to be the head Mouseketeer, but they knew it had to be Walt's idea. So they set Walt up. They brought Jimmie in as a songwriter and had him play "The Pencil Song." As Walt was leaving he said, "You know what? I think we've found our lead Mouseketeer." Jimmie had the job!

jim algar DIRECTOR

We all have blind spots in pronunciation of words. "Hover" was one of Walt's blind spots—he always said, "hoover." Once, I wrote a television lead-in for him and, unthinkingly, dropped in the word "hover." He came down to the stage to record the narration and as he was reading, I heard him say "…hoovered over us." I was in the monitor booth and had to push the control button and my voice came booming inside the booth, like a voice from the heavens. It was a delicate moment. I said, "Walt, gosh, I'm sorry to interrupt you, but that should be 'hovered' not 'hoovered.'"

He kind of snorted and said, "Oh, you and your damn college education."

winston hibler PRODUCER

In the early days, Walt would help write his dialogue. There were certain things he didn't feel were proper to do. He didn't want to talk about himself or praise anything that was personally his product or idea. He said, "I like to talk the way people talk." He never liked stilted dialogue or anything that was too formalized. Walt was a good guy in that he would go along with every joke. He didn't mind being the butt of the joke if it worked for him.

roy e. disney NEPHEW

I wrote the lead-in for the show called *The Legend of Two Gypsy Dogs*, which was to appear on Walt's weekly television show. His lead-in read, "We found this film in Hungary and it was made by a good friend of mine (who he'd never met), Istvan Homoki-Nagy." After Walt saw that name on the TelePrompTer, I got a frantic phone call from the stage saying, "Walt wants you down here right now."

So I went running down and Walt asked, "How do you say that?"

"Istvan Homoki-Nagy (Homokee-Naj)," I replied. He tried saying it three or four times and finally we called the editor, George Gale, who was Hungarian. George came over and Walt asked, "What is this? How do you say this?" George repeated the name and Walt said, "'Istvan,' what is that?"

"In English, that's Steven," George responded.

"Steve! I'll call him Steve!" Walt said. So we changed the line on the TelePrompTer for Walt to read, "This is a film made by my old friend *Steve*, in Hungary."

peter ellenshaw ARTIST

I got instructions to rush my matte painting for *Davy Crockett*, which was scheduled to air on television in three days. During the intense process, Walt came in and observed, "Peter, your standard is slipping."

"Walt," I said, "I can't bring them up to standard in the short amount of time I have to complete them."

"What do you mean?" he asked. I explained to him that we only had three days to finish them.

"You don't listen to these people," he advised. "They'll always push you. Just do the best you can and if they can't have it at that time, then they'll have to put something else on the air in place of *Davy Crockett*. You can't be pushed." He wanted the best out of you and he got it that way.

lillian disney WIFE

On Sunday nights, we would eat in front of the TV. He wanted my reaction to his show. Every time I would take a mouthful of food he would look over and say, "You're not looking! You're not looking!"

roy williams ANIMATOR

Walt was in my office one day when suddenly, he looked up at me and said, "Say, you're fat and funny looking. I'm going to put you on *The Mickey Mouse Club* and call you the Big Mooseketeer!"

roy e. disney NEPHEW

It was always a good idea to give Walt a little wiggle room. He had his own idea of what he was expecting to see and if that wasn't what he got, he was not going to be in a good mood about it. So in a sense he was unpredictable. Sometimes he didn't like things you thought he would and you couldn't even begin to figure out why.

But he always made an effort to tell you why he didn't like it or how to construct something that would work for him. One time, I was working on a TV show and he didn't like what I'd written. It wasn't like, "I hate what you wrote!" He said, "Oh, no, this is what we need to do…" and he built this scene and all of the dialogue. This was vintage Walt—all of this came off the top of his head.

At the end of the meeting we were all smiles. Then I got halfway through rewriting it as Walt described and realized there's a massive hole in the story that I didn't notice when he was explaining it. So I walked in to him and said, "You know, there's a big hole in this thing and it won't work no matter what I do here."

He said, "I know. Fix it." He expected people to do that a lot. He knew you had really valuable stuff, if you could just find a way to link everything together.

donn tatum DISNEY EXECUTIVE

In order to counteract the effect of *Wagon Train*, the network executives came in and said, "We've gotta have action. We gotta have Westerns. We gotta have…" Walt was resisting it. Then, to our surprise, we had a meeting set up and in came Walt wearing a cowboy outfit and two guns. He threw the guns on the table and said, "Okay, you want Westerns, you're gonna have Westerns." He proceeded to recount the whole thing about John Slaughter and Elfego Baca. The network executives' eyes were all bugging out and Walt said, "We're gonna give you the *true* heroes and the *true* West!"

Around 1959, Walt called and said, "Now we want to go to NBC and talk about color." Walt made the presentation himself. He discussed the television program and how he believed it would stimulate the public's interest in the color medium. As he left the meeting, he said, "Fellas, I want this deal. If necessary, I'll stand on my head in Macy's window to get it." There isn't any question that *Walt Disney's Wonderful World of Color* turned out to be an extremely successful program. To Walt, it was not just the inherent promotion of color television sets, but the possibility of producing a first-class family program *in color*.

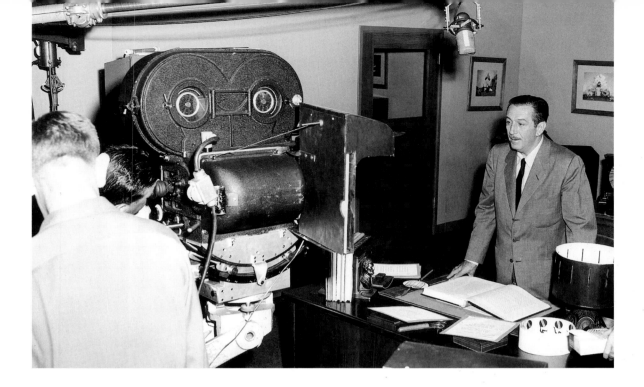

jack speirs WRITER

Walt was on camera with Jack Benny, and before Benny got a chance to do his famous double take, Walt did it perfectly. Benny thought it was hilarious.

diane disney miller DAUGHTER

You could see how he grew between the beginning of television and Disneyland, as a person and a personality. Dad grew as a speaker and in his ability to convey his sense of humor through words. Television didn't change him as a person, but I do think it led to a more polished personality.

marty sklar IMAGINEERING EXECUTIVE

Every time I wrote something for him, I always found a way to use the word "things" because Walt had a marvelous way of making "things" sound so big and magical. For instance, he would say, "And now we're going to create the Pirates of the Caribbean and the pirates are going to burn and sack the whole town! But for our *next* project at Disneyland, we're gonna do some *really* fabulous THINGS."

He just described this fabulous "thing" that was beyond all of our imaginations. Yet, somehow, if he said "things" on camera, that word by itself became much bigger than whatever he was specifically describing at the moment.

diane disney miller DAUGHTER

There was a little park down on Third and La Cienega that he used to take us to quite often. He'd observe people's reactions to various rides and attractions. This was sort of a research project for what would become Disneyland.

He'd see families in the park and say, "There's nothing for the parents to do." The parents would be anxious to leave and the kid would still want to play. He said, "You've got to have a place where the whole family can have fun."

ruth warrick ACTRESS

For the premiere of *Song of the South*, in 1946, we traveled together to New Orleans and then Atlanta. We were having lunch in a restaurant in New Orleans when Walt said, "What this country really needs is an amusement park that families can take their children to. They've gotten so honky tonk with a lot of questionable characters running around and they're not too safe. They're not well kept. I want to have a place that's as clean as anything could ever be and all the people in it are first-class citizens, who are treated like guests."

michael broggie SON OF DISNEY MACHINIST

In 1948, Walt and Ward Kimball went to the Chicago Railroad Fair. From there, they went off to the Henry Ford Museum and Greenfield Village near Dearborn. Between the two experiences, the evolution of Disneyland began.

At the Railroad Fair, Walt ran the historic engines and witnessed corporate sponsorships and fireworks displays over Lake Michigan every night. While at Greenfield Village, there was American history. With his wealth, Henry Ford had amassed a collection of buildings that were of historical and architectural significance, creating a sort of living history museum. At the village, Walt saw buildings that had belonged to America's most prolific inventor, Thomas Edison; the home of dictionary magnate Noah Webster; the Wright Brothers' bicycle shop and even a sternwheeler, Suwanee, that circled a small island in manmade waters. A lot of ideas began to generate in Walt and he started formulating an idea for Mickey Mouse Park, with a Western village, Main Street, and more.

ward kimball ANIMATOR

Initially, he was going to build an amusement park across from the Studio on Riverside Drive. He was thinking of putting in a little half-inch scale railroad that would zigzag its way over to the Studio lot. The track would go through the different soundstages so the riding tourists could see how films were made.

herb ryman ARTIST

I was working at home on a Saturday in 1952, when I received a call from Walt asking me to come over to the Studio. I said, "When?" and he said, "Now. How long will it take you to get here?" I told him twenty minutes and I was on my way. When I got to the Studio, Walt said, "Hi, Herb. We have a new project. It's sort of an amusement park." I asked Walt what he was going to call it and he said, "Disneyland."

Walt described Disneyland. Then he said, "Roy has to go to New York on Monday to raise money for this. We need a plan to show what it will look like. You know, the bankers don't have any imagination."

I said, "Who's going to do the plan?" and Walt said, "You are, Herb." I said, "I don't even know what it's supposed to be," and Walt said, "If I stay here with you and tell you what it is, will you make a drawing?" So the first drawing of Disneyland was done over a Saturday and Sunday.

lillian disney WIFE

I was afraid of Disneyland. So was Roy. But he went ahead. I felt the same way about many things. The short cartoons were successful—why go on? The same with feature cartoons. Walt said he would get stagnant if he didn't do new things.

art linkletter TELEVISION CELEBRITY

I went out to the Disneyland site with him one time. I didn't say what I thought because I didn't want to spoil his enthusiasm. But after we had driven for about an hour south of Los Angeles, into the country and the orange groves, I thought "Geez! Who's gonna come down here?"

bob thomas JOURNALIST

I remember this trip I took with him from the Studio to Disneyland at a time when they were still pulling the orange trees out of Anaheim. We got into Walt's convertible. Walt talked and I listened. I took some notes because he spoke so rapidly of so many ideas that I didn't want to miss anything—new movies coming up, animation, but mostly

he spoke about the Park and his dreams. When we arrived, a group of men were there to greet him.

We got in a Jeep; there was no place to walk. Main Street was blank, there was no castle, just a few orange trees. They were digging out Adventureland and we drove into this pit where the jungle boats were going to be and he acted out the whole routine.

"Giraffes, you can see them in the trees over there and then you come into the hippo pond. Look out! There's a hippo coming right at the boat! And the boat swerves and you get a splash of water. Then you see these natives dancing and holding shrunken heads. And you get into all kinds of hazards—alligators, lions. You go down the rapids until you finally arrive back at civilization."

In Walt's mind, the whole trip was in this hole in the ground. I don't think the imagineers were able to capture the whole experience the way Walt described it. It was unforgettable.

dick irvine IMAGINEER

We used to go to Knott's Berry Farm and the County Fair. You couldn't keep Walt away from these places. At Knott's Berry Farm, we'd measure the width of the walkways, the traffic flow, and study how people moved about. Even at that time, Walt had in the back of his mind how he wanted to move people. He was anxious to just get all of the ideas together. It was helping him gel his concepts, which I think were fluid.

When we started, Walt didn't even know how to read a plan. He would never admit it, but we used to fool him about it. He learned quickly though. Pretty soon he not only could read a plan, but could read it better than all of us.

marvin davis IMAGINEER

The minute Disneyland opened, Walt said, "We're gonna kick ourselves for not buying everything within a radius of ten miles around here." He could visualize the growth.

sharon baird MOUSEKETEER

On the opening day of Disneyland, we (Mouseketeers) were in Walt Disney's apartment above the Main Street Fire Station when the gates of the Park opened for the first time. I was standing next to him at the window, watching the guests come pouring through the gates. When I looked up at him, he had his hands behind his back, a grin from ear to ear, and I could see a lump in his throat and a tear streaming down his cheek. He had realized his dream. I was only twelve years old at the time, so it didn't mean as much to me then. But as the years go by, that image of him becomes more and more endearing.

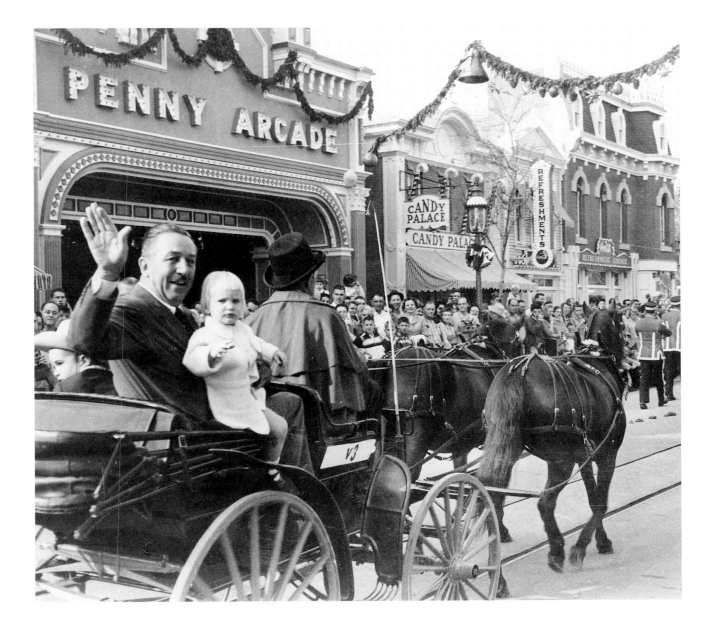

$\mathscr{A}$ KING IN HIS MAGIC KINGDOM

marvin davis IMAGINEER

Walt was the first to go on the attractions. Just like a little kid. He'd get off and giggle or if he didn't like it too well, his eyebrow would go up and he'd say, "Fix this thing and let's get this show on the road."

bill evans LANDSCAPE ARTIST

Walt Disney had the intention that his guests would have a pleasant day at Disneyland, but that they would also leave at the end of their day with some knowledge they didn't have in the morning. He was a stickler for authenticity, good taste, quality, and design. Walt wasn't trying to directly educate people about landscape or architecture or anything else, but he believed his audience would always know the difference between good and bad. To him, Disneyland was a gigantic laboratory and an adventure in public entertainment. Walt kept emphasizing to us that he wanted the public to participate. He wanted them onstage.

john hench ARTIST

I was so astonished by the way Walt would create a kind of live-action cross-dissolve when passing from one area of Disneyland to another. He would even insist on changing the texture of the pavement at the threshold of each new land because he said, "You can get information about a changing environment through the soles of your feet."

marvin davis IMAGINEER

The key to Walt's approach to any kind of design was to consider the environment that was being created for people. He said, "All I want you to think about is when people walk or ride through anything you design, I want them to have smiles on their faces when they leave. Just remember that and that's all I ask you."

dick nunis THEME PARK EXECUTIVE

Walt believed very strongly that the thing that would make his Disneyland unique and different was its people. The quote we still use in our training program today is a Walt quote: "You can design, create, and build the most wonderful place in the world. But it takes people to make the dream a reality."

roy o. disney BROTHER

There was this fellow who worked on the Disneyland railroad train and he handled the public rather curtly. Walt said to one of the employees, "See if you can't give that fellow a better understanding of the business we're in. Cheer him up or if he feels that way, he shouldn't work here. We're selling happiness. We don't like glum pusses or sour faces."

julie andrews ACTRESS

When we first arrived in California, he took me to Disneyland and it was quite amazing to have a personal tour with Walt. In a way, it was like walking with God because all of the visitors wanted to touch him and thank him. They felt like they knew him.

james haught jr. DISNEYLAND EMPLOYEE

We would see him walking around the Park at midnight or four in the morning. He didn't care what time it was. I don't think he lived by the clock; he lived by inspiration.

glynis johns ACTRESS

We visited a department at the studio where the men, who were dressed in overalls, were coming up to Walt every now and again holding a little daffodil or a little rose or some kind of a flower. They were preparing for the opening of the Enchanted Tiki Room.

Walt had told them he wanted each of the different flowers to have a unique sound that was appropriate to the flower. So these chaps were trying to find a little sound for a daffodil or a bluebell or whatever types of flowers they had and they were making these funny sounds for Walt, like Ooh, Ooh! or Bee Boop! Walt was in his element.

bob penfield DISNEYLAND EMPLOYEE

At the Carnation patio on Main Street, there were some people standing watching the parade and Walt was sitting behind them eating with some guests. One of the Park supervisors asked the people standing, "Could you please move so Walt can see?"

Walt heard him and said, "Oh, no. They're paying guests! They're what makes this place go."

bill justice ANIMATOR

One time we were having a meeting and somebody brought up the subject of the character costumes. One of the guys said, "Oh, Walt doesn't want to hear about that."

Walt said, "Wait a minute. They're probably the most important part of the Park. Other people can have their bands, thrill rides, and all this stuff, but we've got the Disney characters and don't think they aren't important! When you see people come in with their children and one of our characters appears, they run to them and get their cameras."

dick van dyke ACTOR

Walt was looking out the window of his apartment, when he saw an employee from Adventureland cross Main Street in Tahitian costume; he got right on the phone! He didn't want the illusion of Main Street U.S.A. spoiled.

hayley mills ACTRESS

He took me and my family to Disneyland and we went on all the best rides. In fact, he took us to the front of the lines. One employee was highly incensed to see this man in his gray suit with his family following after him through the side gate to the front of the line of the Matterhorn. He came running over and said, "Hey, hang on! You can't come through here! You've got to go right around and join the line. Go to the end of the line!"

Walt said, "No, no, no. This is okay. It's all right. I want to take them up to the front of the line here…" and the employee interrupted, "Hang on, mister, hang on! You can't do that. Who do you think you are, Walt Disney?"

"Well, as a matter of fact, I am!" Walt said. This poor employee's face was such a picture.

buddy baker COMPOSER

After Disneyland first opened, we went down there and everything looked a little ratty. It hadn't been kept up. Walt told the engineer who was in charge of maintenance, "I want this place painted."

"Okay, Walt," he said. "We'll do it over the weekend."

"No, I want it painted tonight and finished by morning," ordered Walt. So they called I don't know how many crews of painters and it was painted overnight.

dick irvine IMAGINEER

He knew everything that went into the Park. He knew where every pipe was. He knew the height of every building. He didn't leave a stone unturned, engineering or any of it. He wanted to find out what made things tick.

renie bardeau DISNEYLAND PHOTOGRAPHER

One day, I saw Walt buy a box of popcorn from an employee at the Park. The guy had offered to give it to him, but Walt insisted that the employee had to account for everything at the end of the day and Walt didn't want to mess up the accounting.

Then he wandered over to the Rivers of America and dumped the popcorn into the water for the ducks to eat.

tom nabbe THEME PARK EMPLOYEE

Walt spent a lot of time in Frontierland. I would see him there in the mornings before the Park opened, sitting on the bench in front of the train station. He was kicked back with his arms stretched across the back of the bench taking in the early morning mist and smell of lush vegetation. He seemed content sitting there in his Magic Kingdom.

bo foster SUNKIST EMPLOYEE

When I was in charge of Sunkist Citrus House on Main Street, Walt would come into the shop on Sunday mornings and have his orange juice. He'd put the oranges in the machine and the mechanical arms would slice them, ream them, and pretty soon juice would come roaring out of the spigot.

I put a juicer in his apartment for him and kept his apartment refrigerator stocked with oranges. He'd come into the shop from time to time, however, and say, "Bo, the juice just doesn't taste the same. I'd rather have your juice fresh from the spigot!" I think he liked putting the oranges in the big, old juicing machine.

betty taylor
"GOLDEN HORSESHOE REVUE" STAR

One day I was having breakfast at the Park just before The Swiss Family Treehouse opened for the first time. And there was Walt walking up three steps, then walking down. Then he would walk up four steps and walk back down again. He took the rope railing and shook it. He always tried things out before opening them to the public.

art linkletter TELEVISION CELEBRITY

We'd walk around Disneyland together. And he had a trick that I'd never seen done before. We'd go to his private office and write out our autographs on a little pad of paper, so if people came up to us, we could just tear them off and hand them our signatures, while we kept walking.

One day, Walt and I went into the little magic shop and bought some mustaches and beards and put them on so we wouldn't be recognized. The funny thing was, we were walking along and people were still coming up to us and asking for our autographs and not one of them even asked, "Why are you wearing a beard?"

scotty cribbes DISNEYLAND EMPLOYEE

On the Park's opening day, I was walking down Main Street with a cup of coffee in each hand, when I ran into Walt Disney. He stopped me and I thought I was going to be fired, but he just wanted to know where he could get a cup of coffee.

renie bardeau DISNEYLAND PHOTOGRAPHER

One morning I was sitting in the interior dining room of Hills Bros. Coffee Shop, when Walt walked in and looked around for a place to sit. I was the only one in there and he walked up and asked, "Mind if I sit down?"

"No, of course not, sit right down, Walt." He asked me a couple of questions about the Park. We had met before and it surprised me that he remembered my name.

Suddenly, a waitress showed up and asked "Can I help you, Mr. Disney?"

Walt replied, "Yes, but remember, I'm Walt. There's only one 'mister' in Disneyland and that's *Mr.* Toad."

marty sklar IMAGINEERING EXECUTIVE

In the late 1950s, it cost 24 cents to produce and merchandise the Disneyland souvenir guide, which sold for 25 cents. The company was only making a penny on it and the merchandising people wanted to raise the price. So they went to Walt and made their pitch and he said, no. They were in shock.

"Look," he said. "You don't get it. I don't care about making money on this. What I want is as many of these souvenir guides as possible on people's coffee tables. I want others to see what Disneyland is all about and come for a visit. We'll make our money when they actually come to Disneyland and buy tickets and souvenirs. I don't care about making money on every single item. I want people to visit Disneyland!" Walt was looking at the big picture all the time.

dick nunis THEME PARK EXECUTIVE

We were redoing the Storybook Land attraction and trying to cut its budget. One of the art directors said, "Walt, we can just use regular glass rather than stained glass."

Walt said something profound, "Look, the thing that's going to make Disneyland unique and different is the detail. If we lose the detail, we lose it all."

jack lindquist DISNEYLAND EXECUTIVE

Walt wanted to put in the Matterhorn, Monorail, and Submarines for summer 1959, but his brother had other ideas. Roy said we were just getting out of the hole and we'd have to wait two or three years. Then he left for Europe to raise money for motion pictures.

Two days after he left, Walt called WED and said, "We're going to build the Matterhorn, Monorail, and Submarines."

WED said, "But Roy said we can't afford it."

"We're going to build them," he said. "Roy can figure out how to pay for them when he gets back."

ray bradbury AUTHOR

Walt was redoing Tomorrowland and next time I had lunch with him, I said, "Walt, I'd like to help," because I had helped create the United States Pavilion at the New York World's Fair. "Why not hire me to consult on the new Tomorrowland?"

"Ray, it's no use," Walt said.

"Why?" I said.

"Because you're a genius and I'm a genius," Walt said. "We'd kill each other the first week!"

"That's the nicest turndown I've ever had," I said.

john hench ARTIST

Walt never felt better than when things were under construction at Disneyland. When things were torn up, it was hardhat time. God, he loved that! He got kind of nervous when things were static. He had a sense of destiny about it all—it was gonna grow…it was gonna grow bigger!

joe fowler DISNEYLAND EXECUTIVE

He used to come down to the Park quite frequently during its first year. He used to say, "You know, Joe, I come down here to get a real rest from the humdrum of making pictures at the Studio. This is my real amusement. This is where I relax."

xavier atencio IMAGINEER

We mocked up the pirate ride auction scene in a warehouse for Walt to see. Then we rigged up a dolly with a chair and pushed him through at about the speed of the boats. As we got to the scene, the sound was playing and it was a great cacophony of pirate voices and music. I said, "Sorry, Walt. It's hard to understand what they're saying."

"Oh, hell," he said. "It's like a cocktail party. You tune into one conversation and then into another. Each time guests go through, they'll hear something new and different." Of course, he was right.

diane disney miller DAUGHTER

When we went to Paris, Dad went off on his own and came back with boxes and boxes of these little windup toys. He wound them all up and put them on the floor of the room and just sat and watched them. You know, the dog that rolls over and stuff like that.

He said, "Look at that movement with just a simple mechanism." He was studying; he could see Audio-Animatronics. We thought he was crazy.

john hench ARTIST

Shortly after Disneyland opened, one of the art directors began complaining about guests cutting through a planted area of the Park. And Walt said, "Now, wait a minute! A path like that isn't created by an occasional person cutting through, but many people cutting through. You've got to realize that people do this because they have a good reason to walk through there. Don't fence it off. Pave it for them!"

dick irvine IMAGINEER

Walt could never get hold of Tomorrowland. He always said, "The minute we do Tomorrowland, it's today and past."

harriet burns ARTIST

We built three different style models of the Haunted Mansion to let Walt pick from. We kept putting the scary-looking Addams Family-style model up in front, but Walt always picked the style of Haunted Mansion that exists in the Park today. Finally, we said to him, "Walt, when we think of a haunted mansion we think of a haunted look."

"No, no," he said. "The haunting is on the *inside*. I want everything at Disneyland nice, clean and attractive."

john hench ARTIST

When Disneyland first opened, Walt told us to get down there at least twice a month. He said, "Stand in line with people and for God's sake, don't go off the lot to eat like you guys have been doing. You eat at the Park and listen to people!"

bob gurr IMAGINEER

Sometimes he'd just come down to somebody's room and sit there. He wouldn't say anything, just sit there. You could see when he had an idea. One time I spotted that eyebrow go up and he said, "Bobby, do you know what we haven't got? We haven't got an omnibus on Main Street in Disneyland! I've got a dinky toy in my office, I'll be right back." When he came back he gave me the toy as reference. Then he left and a little while later a lady called up and said, "The accounting charge number for the omnibus project is…" Within an hour!

A year later, he came in, sat in the office again and I said, "Walt, you know there's something we haven't got on Main Street. We don't have a fire engine!"

"No, we don't!" he said. So he left and within the hour the accounting office rang, "The fire engine accounting number is…" I like that story because everybody knew that the rule was that Walt suggested everything, you weren't to suggest anything. Here was the exception.

john hench ARTIST

He'd often say, "What you need is a weenie, which says to people 'come this way.' People won't go down a long corridor unless there's something promising at the end. You've got to have something that beckons them to 'walk this way.'"

dick nunis THEME PARK EXECUTIVE

Billy Graham came to the Park in the early 1960s. He'd never been to Disneyland before and Walt escorted him around. I was with them to make sure everything went all right. We got off the Jungle Cruise and Billy stopped in the middle of Adventureland and said, "Gosh, what a fantastic world! What a marvelous fantasy world."

Walt said, "Billy, look around you at all the people. All the nationalities. All the colors. All the languages. All of them are smiling. All of them are having fun together. Billy, *this* is the *real* world. The fantasy's outside."

marty sklar IMAGINEERING EXECUTIVE

One of the reasons Walt went in on the World's Fair was
that he was still building Disneyland and needed more
money to accomplish the kinds of things he wanted to
create. His plan was to bring the shows back from the Fair
to Disneyland and that's how we got It's a Small World, The
Carousel of Progress, Great Moments with Mr. Lincoln, and
the dinosaur diorama along the train route.

donn tatum DISNEY EXECUTIVE

Walt called us together. He said, "Look, there's going to
be a big fair in New York and big companies are going to
be spending a heck of a lot of money building exhibits.
They won't know what they want to do; they won't know
why they're doing it except they just feel they have to keep
up with the Joneses. Some of them are going to recognize
the need for the kind of service we can offer because they

want to have something that will stand out from the competition.

"It's a great opportunity for us because we're trying to promote the idea of a place like Disneyland. Let's present ourselves and be very willing to render our services to build attractions. It will help us. We'll learn a lot and it will give us a chance to develop technology we're working on." He was very, very farsighted about it. At that time, the Audio-Animatronics technology was bursting forth and he was very engrossed in that.

floyd gottfredson ARTIST

They came back to Walt and said, "Audio-Animatronics can't be done. There's just no way you can do that."

"Damn it!" he said. "If you can visualize it, if you can dream it, there's some way to do it. Now keep after it until we get it!"

bob gurr IMAGINEER

Walt pointed at this terrible pile of junk that was supposed to be Abraham Lincoln and said to me, "I want twice as many motions and nothing shaking." At this time, no human robots existed worth a dime. For Walt to choose to recreate a President of the United States was about as risky an idea as he could get.

A short time later, he asked if it would help the process if he got an actor in costume and had him present Lincoln's speech. "Then you can film the performance and play it over again as you fine tune him," he said. I agreed that it would be helpful; I didn't know what Walt had in mind.

We met on a Saturday and there was a small crew there to run the lights, camera, and sound. Royal Dano performed for us and I thought his first reading, which lasted ten to fifteen minutes, was good. But Walt jumped up, "No, no, no!" So Royal performed it again, but he was draggy this time. At the end, Walt again said, "No! You haven't got it, damn it!" Royal sighed and started the long speech again. This time I thought his performance was terrible; he was obviously tired and had lost energy.

Then Walt jumped up and started directing us in singing "The Battle Hymn of the Republic." This technical event suddenly became very emotional. As I describe it, I still get choked up. All along..., Walt saw this show in his head and he knew how he wanted it to sound and to be performed. He wanted Royal Dano's performance to sound weary and worn. Little did we know, at the time, this would be the audio used in the final attraction. Walt had motives behind what he was doing.

jim algar DIRECTOR

The Abraham Lincoln figure was the most sophisticated Audio-Animatronics mechanism we had ever attempted. As the deadline approached for the New York World's Fair, however, fuses would blow out and wires would get crossed and the thing wasn't working right. It was the most nerve-wracking thing. One night, Marc Davis turned to me and said, "Do you suppose God is mad at Walt for creating man in his own image?"

donn tatum DISNEY EXECUTIVE

There was a quality about Walt I admired very much. He tended to "accentuate the positive." I had a few occasions, during the New York World's Fair, when something he wanted to do had failed. He'd take the setback and immediately start to say why that was an advantage. He would say, "That's a good thing because now we can do this…" and he would immediately turn his mind to another track.

alice davis COSTUME DESIGNER

Walt, Admiral Joe Fowler, and the CEO of PepsiCo were in a boat going through the It's A Small World attraction at the New York World's Fair. Marc and I were walking over the bridge as the boat was coming toward us. Walt saw me and asked, "Alice, how come you put long pantaloons on the Can-Can girls?"

"You told me you wanted a family show!" I said. They all broke up.

richard sherman SONGWRITER

We never dreamed the song "It's a Small World" would ever become as popular as it did. The day we first demonstrated it at WED, Walt drove us back to the Studio. Bob and I remarked about how "The attraction is sponsored by UNICEF. It's a good cause so why don't we donate our royalties to them?"

Walt stopped the car, turned around and reprimanded us, "Don't you ever do that! This song is gonna see your kids through college. UNICEF will make plenty of money out of the pavilion. You want to make a donation? Do that! But don't give away your royalties!" He alone knew it would live on and on; we had no idea how far ahead he was looking. Then, two years later he said, "You know that song…we're taking the whole damn attraction and putting it in Disneyland, permanently. Now, do you see what I meant?" and walked away.

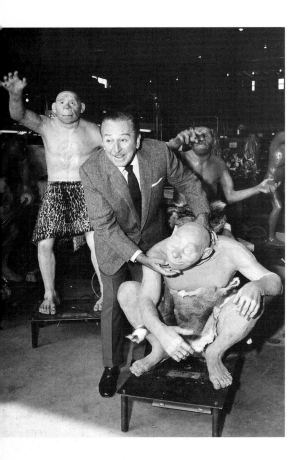

marc davis ANIMATOR

We were at the New York World's Fair when people began to discover Walt Disney. Little girls, teenagers wearing sweatshirts, blue jeans, bobby sox, and tennis shoes came running up, "Oh, gosh, Mr. Disney would you sign this?" He was very gentle, very understanding with them. He signed four or five autographs and then reached out and took a girl's hands and said, "Look, honey, I'm going to get mobbed here. I can't sign anymore," and she started screaming, "He touched me! He touched me!"

jack speirs WRITER

Walt didn't like meetings. He told me that a meeting was a bunch of people pooling their common ignorance. So when I was writing the General Electric Carousel of Progress show for the World's Fair, about three or four times a month the honchos from General Electric would fly out to hold a meeting to discuss the project. Nothing would ever get settled in those meetings. Walt finally came in and stood at the head of the table and said, "All right gentlemen, what I want you to do is go down to the Coral Room and have a good lunch. Then I want you to go back to Burbank Airport and get in your Grumman Gulf Stream and fly back east where you came from and stay there until I've got something I want you to see. Then, I'll call *you*. Thank you, gentlemen" and he turned around and left. So did GE.

alice davis COSTUME DESIGNER

I was working on the It's a Small World attraction when Walt came in. I was dressing some of the dolls and he said, "Alice, come down here. I want to show you something."

So I came down and he took me by the arm and walked me over to a Mercury station wagon. In the back seat of this car sat the grandmother from the General Electric show in her shawl.

"Isn't she cute," he said. "I'm taking her on a commercial airline to New York. I'm not going to ship her to New

York in a box. I'm putting her in a wheelchair and going to wheel her into the first-class section of the plane."

He was just like a little kid with the greatest toy of all time. He was so excited about this prank he was going to play that he had to tell somebody about it. I heard he took her on the plane and everyone said, "Oh, isn't she a sweet little old lady."

dick nunis THEME PARK EXECUTIVE

I honestly didn't understand why Walt wanted to go to the World's Fair. Once I learned about Project X, however, it was clear to me. He wanted to see if his type of entertainment would be accepted on the East Coast and if his creative people could compete with the world designers. All four of our shows at the Fair were top attractions.

marty sklar IMAGINEERING EXECUTIVE

There were some things he was influenced by. I know he had a book in his office by architect Victor Gruen called *Out of a Fair, a City.* That book was in his office a long time while he was planning EPCOT. It's all about how a World's Fair can be used as an infrastructure for a city.

UNFINISHED BUSINESS: EPCOT, WALT DISNEY WORLD AND CALARTS

art linkletter TELEVISION CELEBRITY

I was at a birthday party at his house and he took me aside and said, "Artie, I just wanna ask your opinion about something. I'm thinking about doing a Disneyland in Florida. Whaddaya think about it?"

I said, "I wouldn't do it."

"Why not?"

"Because, Walt," I said, "Disneyland is the only park of its kind in the entire world. It's like the pyramids in Egypt, Niagara Falls, or the Grand Canyon. If there's two, then it isn't unique anymore."

He said, "Yeah, but I've learned so much. All the things we did there were just like an experimental laboratory. In Florida, I could get a lot of land. There'd be nobody crowding in on me and doing things I didn't like right next to me. I can correct all those things."

I said, "In that case, I change my mind. You're not doing it to just make more money?"

He said, "No. I'm doing it because I want to do it *better*."

dick nunis THEME PARK EXECUTIVE

He called me up to his apartment at Disneyland and said, "Dick, we're going to do something big. We're going to call it Project X and we're going to have all the land we can imagine. We're just going to keep buying land."

On one occasion, we had a small meeting and there was a large parcel of land in Orlando and Walt said, "Buy it!"

Roy said, "But, Walt we already own 12,000 acres. Do we have the money?" The price was like $100 an acre.

"Roy," Walt said, "how would you like to own 12,000 acres around Disneyland right now?"

And Roy said, "Buy it!"

marty sklar IMAGINEERING EXECUTIVE

Walt hated the forest of signs and motels that popped up around Disneyland. It bothered him that he didn't have enough money, at the time, to buy land to protect himself from that kind of development. He wanted to make sure in Florida that nothing like that would ever happen again.

kelvin bailey WALT'S PILOT

We flew Walt down around Tampa. He told me, "I want to go to Orlando tomorrow morning and I don't want anybody to know. I want to be ultra secret about it."

The next morning, I took him to Orlando and we were met there at the airport by these Land Rover vehicles. He said, "Kel, why don't you come on along." I didn't know what was going on, but "Yes, sir!"

We drove ten or twenty miles and we got to this nasty, wasted country. Water, swamps, jungle, alligators. I thought, "What are we doing here?" I was dressed in a suit and tie.

He said, "Kel, this is going to be my next Disneyland." I thought, he's got to be out of his mind—This is *nothing*! Water up to our knees! You couldn't have given me the land.

But, everything was so vivid to him. He pointed and said, "Main Street here, Tomorrowland there, Fantasyland over here." Nothing but swamp and alligators. But he could envision the *whole* thing.

"We're going to drain it all," he said. "We'll have pumps going all the time. Everything's going to be underground. But this time we're not going to make the same mistake we made at Anaheim. We're going to buy the whole countryside!"

I thought, "Walt, you're cracking up."

dick nunis THEME PARK EXECUTIVE

He said, "We've got to study the land" and the first report done on the Florida project was where you should build and where you shouldn't build. Walt was so smart. He said, "We've got to put Disneyland, which everybody will know, at the very upper end of the property because that will be the weenie." Then whatever we build after that, the public will have to drive by to get to the Park.

marty sklar IMAGINEERING EXECUTIVE

When we were making plans to go into Florida, Joe Potter said, "Walt, I've been down in Florida as your representative and those people there think you can do anything. In fact, they think you can walk on water." Walt looked at him, got up and walked out the door. We could hear his footsteps going down the hall. Then we could hear his footsteps coming back. He opened the door, popped his head back in the room and said, "I've tried that," closed the door, and left.

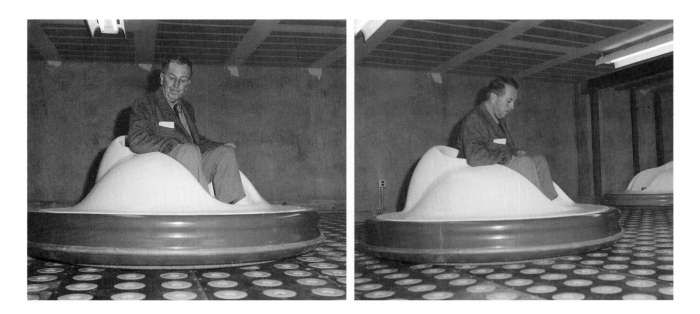

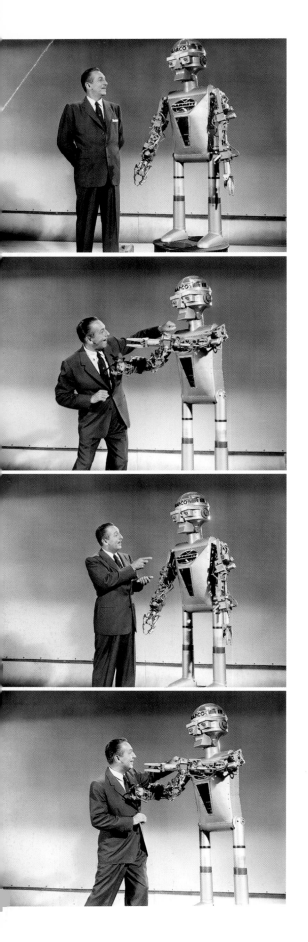

marvin davis IMAGINEER

During some of the early plot plans I was working on for Disneyland, I thought we were constricting the front entrance by making it rather pear-shaped. I said, "Walt, we're squeezing ourselves a little bit on either side of Main Street and I think we maybe should expand this a bit." But he was in love with the design.

Ten years later, when we were in some kind of a conference on the Florida project, I made a point that we weren't allowing enough space around a particular development. Walt said, "By God! Maybe you're right. You know the only mistake I can ever remember making (he was joking in a cocky way) was when I didn't listen to you about enlarging the area on either side of Main Street." We hadn't discussed that in ten years!

Walt had been asked, I'm sure almost begged, by people all over the world to repeat Disneyland in any number of different places. He always steadfastly refused to do another Disneyland because he said he had done the best park he knew how to do and why would he want to repeat himself? He said, "There are too many things in the world to do that are different and new and more of a challenge to me."

The only reason I'm sure he ever decided to tackle Disney World was because of its connection to EPCOT. With all the problems and struggles that the world is going through with urban societies, I guess he decided to tackle the problem, himself, in a way he thought he could.

It was not his philosophy to build a city that solved all of the problems of urban living, but to create a laboratory for American industry to experiment in solving problems, such as housing and traffic problems. He figured he would create a community in which ideas and philosophies could be tested out, not just physical things.

In other words, he really wanted to open this up to American industry so that it could expand and use all of its research and development programs, that they might not be able to try out because of archaic ordinances and government rules.

He was successful in getting the Florida legislature to grant us the privilege of writing our own building and zoning codes and ordinances so we would have all the powers and authorities that are granted to counties.

ron miller SON-IN-LAW

The doctor said, "Walt, you're not going to be able to work fourteen hours a day like you've been doing." I think right then and there Walt thought, "Well, what is most important to work on? Disney World!" He realized that Disney World and EPCOT were not something he could build in just a year or two.

He said, "I'm gonna stick with Disney World and EPCOT. I'll read scripts and tell you whether or not to go with them, but I just can't be as active as I used to be."

roy e. disney NEPHEW

I've always thought he considered the Studio and WED prototypes for CalArts. He wanted to create a school where everybody's rubbing off on everybody else and where one type of artist is codependent on every other type.

diane disney miller DAUGHTER

Dad felt very, very truly that he had something to give education. He believed that you could educate and entertain at the same time. They don't have to be two separate things and that education can be a pleasant, entertaining, enlightening experience. He believed they went hand in hand.

roy o. disney BROTHER

Walt could never tolerate the guy who was self-satisfied with his art. I heard him again and again say to fellows, "Look, you're capable of a hell of a lot better work. You can't just get a certain degree of proficiency and sit there all your life. You have to keep at it all the time!"

He'd compel them to go to Chouinard Art School. The guys who would revolt or rebel, they didn't last very long. They left with chips on their shoulders, as though Walt were some kind of an ogre.

Walt was obsessed with the idea that, in life, you continually go to school. You never reach any plateau of finished perfection. And he practiced that, too, in everything he did. But there were a lot of people who looked for alibis for their own inefficiencies or laziness and they were the ones who grumbled and fell out with Walt.

les clark ANIMATOR

Walt ran the Studio like a university. We were learning all the time and a few of us were going to art school at night. Walt would drive us there and pick us up later. That was when there was just a handful of us. He started training programs and invited interesting and inspirational people to speak to us, like Frank Lloyd Wright.

joe grant STORY ARTIST

I was surprised that with his limited education, he got so involved with classical music. But Walt hankered after education. *Fantasia* was his musical education: the people he hired were for a purpose. The fact that they were from a university was big stuff to him because he absorbed from them, as well as from authors like Aldous Huxley who came to the Studio. If they told him an anecdote and he told it over again, it was much more interesting the way he told it.

ollie johnston ANIMATOR

For a guy who only went to the eighth grade, Walt educated himself beautifully. His vocabulary was good. I only heard him get sore about a big word once in a story meeting. Everyone was sitting around talking and Ted Sears said, "Well, I think that's a little too strident."

Walt said, "What the hell are you trying to say, Ted?" He hadn't heard that word before.

tommie wilck WALT'S SECRETARY

We went through a period of time when he decided we were going to investigate new words. We were learning a word a day. Walt would think of a word and then I would find the origin of the word and the Latin derivative and its meaning. We had big discussions.

roy o. disney BROTHER

From the very beginning of Walt's career, he was interested in using the cartoon as an educational medium. There was a man in Kansas City, a dentist, that every now and then would get a grant of $500 from a Kansas City merchant to make films about dentistry, so Walt made two or three reels for him. As time went on, we had a national committee of five leading educators working with us for three or four years trying to find a way to make *educational* pictures. We gave it serious study, but one day, Walt concluded, "Oh, to hell with it. From now on, let's make 'educational' a dirty word around here. Let's just stick to entertainment—we'll give them sugar-coated educational films!"

t. hee DIRECTOR

He called me one evening over at WED. I guess it was about six o'clock and we talked for a full hour. He talked to me; I didn't talk to him. I just said, "Yes, sir."

He was wound up and said, "I want to talk to you about CalArts (California Institute of the Arts). I want people to graduate from there really able to do things. I don't want a lot of theorists. I want to have a school that turns out people that know all the facets of filmmaking. I want them to be capable of doing anything needed to make a film—photograph it, direct it, design it, animate it, record it, whatever. That's what I want. Hell, I've hired theorists, and they don't have any knowledge I can use. I want to have everyone in that school come out capable of going in and doing a job. These dilettantes who come out with pseudo-knowledge, they give me a pain. I want it so that if an actor is needed, they can get an actor right out of the school. If a musician is needed, they can go to the music department and find musicians who can compose music."

harrison "buzz" price
RESEARCH CONSULTANT

He wanted to build that school! It was the most pervasive objective in a man's mind that I've ever run into. He was very close to the evolution of CalArts, he was passionate all the way. He said, "This is the thing I'm going to be remembered for."

marc davis ANIMATOR

Walt felt people would come to CalArts from around the world. In other words, he hoped someday to make this 100 percent scholarship. This was his dream, to attract the outstanding talent and put them in this environment where they experience absolutely everything. He was thinking of this as a professional and *not* an ivory tower institution.

harrison "buzz" price
RESEARCH CONSULTANT

An educator? No. I don't think Walt thought of himself as an amusement park builder either. He was fascinated with what you could make out of big ideas; he wanted the product. Walt was a colossal thinker.

marc davis ANIMATOR

CalArts was in the works and Walt wanted to get artists like Salvador Dali and Pablo Picasso to spend three months at the school as guest professors. He even said, "Hell, maybe I could teach a class there!" Then he looked at me, frowned and added, "I don't mean to teach *drawing*, for God's sake! But I'm a damn good story man! I could teach *story*!"

harrison "buzz" price
RESEARCH CONSULTANT

On the last day I ever saw him, we had a board meeting at which he presented CalArts in model form. Then he took me and Lulu Mae Von Hagen into the side room and handed me a box full of all the reports I had written, which had been stored under his desk. He looked at the two of us and said, "Look after my school." I think he knew he was doomed. I have never welshed; in the thirty-six years I've served on its board, I've never even thought of leaving the school.

WHAT

DREAMS

MAY COME

ON DECEMBER 5, 1966,

Walter Elias Disney turned sixty-five in St. Joseph's Hospital in Burbank, California. He was too ill to celebrate. Only a month before, doctors had removed his left lung. Growing weaker by the day, Walt was a fading shadow of his former energetic self.

During the previous few years, he had developed some chronic ailments. He had a sinus condition that took him to a doctor every Tuesday. After his sinuses were drained, he spent much of the remaining day coughing in his office.

Like clockwork, he came down with a bad cold every winter and even developed walking pneumonia on several occasions. Other ailments included a kidney condition and severe facial pain, caused by a bad tooth.

By early 1966, his old polo injury to the neck began shooting pain down his back and into his left leg. The pain affected the way he walked, so much so that his secretary Tommie Wilck recalled, "You'd have sworn he'd been drinking. He *never* drank during the day." Rumors were circulating around the Studio by the time he finally went to see a doctor. X-rays showed further calcification of his old neck injury, and an operation was prescribed to relieve Walt of the debilitating pain.

On Wednesday, November 2, he entered the hospital for more tests, when a spot the size of a walnut was detected on his left lung. Surgery was scheduled for the following Monday.

Walt didn't want word to spread to the public; he feared the company's stock would plummet, squelching his latest and greatest plans—CalArts and EPCOT. He told a few intimates, while casually dismissing his illness to others.

Tommie brought his mail to him every day, creating the pretense for Walt, as much as for Studio employees and stockholders, that he was well enough to keep busy. He even called bedside meetings about *The Happiest Millionaire*, as it concluded production.

His daughter Diane had decided it was best just to pop in and out of his room rather than linger as if on a death watch. It's still unclear whether Walt actually knew he was dying. Perhaps, like everybody else, he was hoping he would beat the odds.

Most employees knew Walt wasn't well; word had even filtered down to Disneyland employees in Anaheim. Some sensed death was only a matter of time, while others thought Walt would soon bounce back to work again. Some even speculated if Walt were confined to a wheelchair, what sort of a marvelous device would he come up with to get around in. To many of his staff, Walt was the tent pole that could never be hewn down.

On Monday, November 21, two weeks after his surgery, Walt checked out of the hospital and went straight to the Studio. He walked the lot and talked with many people and even came in to work the next day. People marveled at Walt's fortitude, particularly since it was obvious he wasn't well.

On Wednesday, November 23, he went to see some dailies. When he didn't return to the office in a timely manner, Tommie called the front gate and discovered he had gone home early. When she called his home, Lillian Disney explained that Walt had gone to bed, exhausted from his activities.

Walt spent a quiet Thanksgiving with his family at Diane and Ron's, in Encino. The next day he and Lillian flew to their home at Smoke Tree Ranch in Palm Springs, where he was determined to stay until he was better. By November 30, however, Walt was back at St. Joseph's Hospital in Burbank, where he remained until his death the morning of December 15, 1966. His death certificate records the cause of death as acute circulatory collapse.

Quickly and quietly, his grief-stricken family held a small, private service at Forest Lawn Cemetery in Glendale, where his ashes were laid to rest. Soon, a rumor began circulating among employees. Walt had always explored cutting-edge technology and at that time, a new science called cryogenics was on the horizon. As they coped with their loss, employees began to speculate "what if?" What if Walt had himself frozen until a cure for cancer was developed? Soon, "what if" fell by the wayside and wishful thinking transformed into Hollywood lore.

More enduring than the legend and lore is Walt's legacy. His premature death impacted not just those who knew him, but those who knew of him. The entire world mourned because a bright light had gone dark and a beloved voice had gone silent. More than thirty years after his death, however, Walt's life still resonates. The impressions he left on those who knew him were profound and lasting, while his visions as recorded in theme parks, education, futuristic communities, and on film and television will live forever. As long as there is imagination…the world will always Remember Walt.

A BRAVE FACE

ollie johnston ANIMATOR

We knew something was wrong and we all worried about him. In our last story meeting together, before Walt went into the hospital, Milt Kahl asked him, "Are you worried?"

"You're damned right I am," he answered.

lucille martin WALT'S SECRETARY

Shortly before he went into the hospital, at the end of a workday, Walt sat talking to Tommie and me about CalArts and EPCOT. Walt was unusually tired and as he got up said, "Sometimes I just feel like chucking it all." Then he looked over at me and said, "But Lucille and her girls need me."

"That we do," I said, and Walt smiled. I've always cherished his saying that.

jack speirs WRITER

Shortly after I heard Walt had to go back to the hospital for further examination, I got stuck with him in the elevator. He was wearing a cardigan sweater that was the most flaming yellow you have ever seen. He was in one of his unsociable moods.

I was on one side of the elevator and he was on the other and I was looking at him and he looked up and we locked eyes. Under those circumstances, you've got to say something; it's one of those things. So I said, "I'd like to wrestle you for that sweater, Walt."

He rumbled, "What are you working on, Speirs?"

"Charlie the Lonesome Cougar."

"Be a good show," he commented.

"Yep, if I ever get it finished."

We got off the elevator. Walt's office was down at one end of the building and my office was right across the hall from the elevator. I had just opened the door and stepped inside when I heard, "Hey, Jackson!" I stepped back into the hallway and Walt walked back and said, "When I get out of the hospital, I *will* wrestle you for the sweater." He slapped me on the shoulder and walked away. That's the last time I ever saw him.

dean jones ACTOR

While we were shooting *Blackbeard's Ghost*, I had heard that Walt had been across the street at St. Joseph's Hospital having an operation on his neck. One day, after the director yelled "cut," I glanced up and right behind the camera stood Walt. He looked terrible. His cheeks were sunken and his face looked thin and extremely tired. I looked at him in shock.

When I realized how I had reacted, I walked over trying to cover my feelings with a smile. "Walt, how are you? How's your neck?" He said, "Neck, hell, they took out my left lung." I was speechless. Normally, Walt would keep the ball rolling in a conversation. This time, he didn't—he just stood there. I was thinking cancer and "Walt's dying"—all these thoughts went racing through my mind. Just as I was called back to the set, he said, "I'm going to Palm Springs."

I paused, then said, "Walt, can you wait around a minute. We're gonna finish this short take. I want to tell you something."

I had no idea what I was gonna say to him—I was stalling. I just knew I wanted to say something of value to this man who had meant so much to me and the world. I went back to work, but kept blowing takes. I blew about seven takes on a very simple scene. I couldn't concentrate; couldn't get it straight. When I finally got one right, I walked back to where Walt had been, but he was gone.

diane disney miller DAUGHTER

One time, when he had a kidney stone, he thought he was dying. Of course, it's terribly painful. We came into the hospital room just after he found out it was only a kidney stone and he said, "I'm going to live!" Then he picked up the phone, called the Studio manager and said, "Get some buffalo and a pony on the ranch for my grandchildren." When he knew he had cancer, however, he kept it to himself. He must have known.

robert sherman COMPOSER

My brother and I ran into Walt in the hall. He looked ill and sort of shrunken. He was talking to director Norman Tokar and then looked at us. He saw the concern on our faces, gave us a smile and said, "Keep up the good work, fellows." It was the first time he said anything like that to us. He never referred to anything we did as good. He usually said, "That'll work."

ron miller SON-IN-LAW

When he was in the hospital I came in with Diane and Lilly and he said to the nurse, "I want you to meet my son."

She said, "You mean son-in-law."

"No," he said, "my *son*." It's the greatest thing that's ever been said to me.

lillian disney WIFE

We had a room next to his in the hospital. He was glad to see us, but he wanted a professional to tend to him—a doctor. The day before he died, he seemed so much better. I trusted the doctors. I really didn't know he was going to go. Neither did he. We had a trip planned for his recovery.

Once, he looked up from the hospital bed, saw all the doctors and said, "Do you fellows know what you're doing?" I think he told the doctors what to do like he told everyone else. He hated illness.

ron miller SON-IN-LAW

We went to see Walt after the operation. He said he thought he had the cancer licked. He was full of confidence. I think the thing that really helped him was a telegram that John Wayne had sent when he heard that Walt had his lung removed. It said, "Welcome to the club. The only problem is height." In other words—altitude. Walt carried that telegram with him; it meant a lot to him.

suzanne pleshette ACTRESS

The morning he came out of the hospital, he came onto our set. We were filming *Blackbeard's Ghost*. He looked so gray and yellow, yet still had a sparkle in his eyes. He must have been in terrible pain. I knew it was coming. If you've ever seen anybody with cancer, you know that color.

He said, "Come out from behind that desk. I wanna see if you're wearing a mini-skirt."

I said, "You just want to see my thighs, you devil you." Those were the last words we spoke. I gave him a big hug and went home that night and cried and cried.

marc davis ANIMATOR

I was in my office and this crowd of people came walking down the hall with Walt. He got to my doorway, stopped and said, "You guys go on, I want to talk with Marc for a few minutes."

You could see the impact the surgery had had on him. He was awfully tired and kinda thin, and as he sat down, I said, "Boy, they sure knocked the weight off you," because he had always patted me on the stomach and said, "Hey, this has gotta go."

So I showed him some drawings of what would become the Country Bear Jamboree at Disneyland and designs for

the Mineral King Resort. I had found with Walt that he was like a child at Christmas. If you had things to show him or another present for him to open, he was happy. Finally, he turned and said, "I think I'd better get back to the Studio."

As he left, I stepped outside my office door and watched him walk down the hall. He got about forty feet away from me and all of a sudden stopped and turned and said, "Goodbye, Marc."

"Goodbye" was a word he *never* used. He'd say, "Let's get together later."

dick nunis THEME PARK EXECUTIVE

Everybody was so amazed at how quick Walt came out of the hospital and back to work at WED. He was calling meetings and talking about the future. I think he was trying to instill the vision as a road map.

winston hibler PRODUCER

I saw him the Monday he came back from the hospital. He was quite weak and drawn. During the course of our conversation, however, his great vitality came back and his voice got firmer and firmer. He said, "I had a scare, Hib. I'm okay, but I may be off my feet for a while. Now, I'm gonna be getting over this and I want to get into Florida. You guys gotta carry some of this load here. But if you get a real problem and you get stuck or something, why, I'm here."

kelvin bailey WALT'S PILOT

While flying to Palm Springs, which took only twenty minutes, he came up to the cockpit and said, "Kel, I've been at old St. Joe's Hospital for some time. I'm a sick boy. But I'm going to Palm Springs and stay there until I get better. I'll call you then. I don't know when, but stand by for the call."

I assumed it would be weeks or months. Two or three days later, the phone rang. "Kel? This is Wa-a-a-l-t." His voice was so fragile, so dilapidated, I hardly recognized him. "Come and get me."

At Palm Springs airport, the car drove up. Lilly got out and had to help Walt out. He couldn't do it alone. There was a stairway leading up to the plane and he had to put his hands on both rails. He went straight to St. Joseph's from the Burbank airport.

roy e. disney NEPHEW

The last time I saw Walt was about two or three days before he went. He was just so gaunt. He was unshaven, scraggly and gray. He looked up at me and said, "Whatever I've got, *don't* get it." To the end, I'm not sure the doctors actually told him, "Walt, you've got lung cancer; you're dying."

diane disney miller DAUGHTER

The last time I saw Dad, he was very uncomfortable. We felt he didn't like people hanging around all the time. When he had moments of great pain or felt something that he couldn't control, he'd get very upset and would rather be alone then.

patty disney NIECE

One of the nurses at St. Joseph's Hospital left us a note. She wrote, "I took care of Walt in his final days and just want you to know that the poor man was so fearful."

joe fowler DISNEYLAND EXECUTIVE

His brother Roy called me maybe two nights before Walt died. I was at home and he said, "Joe, I just wanted to tell you, I've been over to see Walt and he's just wonderful. He's planning Disney World on the squares of the ceiling in his hospital room. He's planning and his spirits are great. I'm so encouraged."

ron miller SON-IN-LAW

When Walt was ill he said, "If I could live for fifteen more years, I would surpass everything I've done over the past forty years."

GOODBYE SO SOON

harriet burns ARTIST

Bill Cottrell was at my desk when he got the phone call from upstairs and they put him through to my number. I said, "It's for you, Bill."

When he hung up he turned to me and said, "Walt Disney just died."

"That's not possible," I said.

"Don't say a word," he instructed, and I didn't. I didn't have to—everybody's radios blasted the news within minutes.

marty sklar IMAGINEERING EXECUTIVE

Nothing had been formally prepared to give to the media in case he died. I was called that morning and asked to write a statement for Roy. I'm still resentful of it because somebody should have written that in advance—after all, we had to try to sum up his life.

This was hard for me to write. Roy refused to talk. I couldn't understand why Walt's death was hitting me so hard. His death hurt me, in many ways, more than when my father died. I never had to think like my father. Having written words for Walt to speak for so long, I had to try to get in his head and think like him and use the words that he would use. It was very emotional for me in a different way than my father's death had affected me.

xavier atencio IMAGINEER

He died on December 15, which was the traditional day I would go out and buy my Christmas tree. After the news broke, we were sent home from work. I went out and bought my Christmas tree and when I returned home, sat down and just bawled because it had hit me that he was gone.

I remember getting all of these holiday greeting cards that year. So many of my friends, even those from Europe whom I had met during the war, wrote notes of condolences to me as though someone in my family had died.

karen dotrice ACTRESS

I was back in England and had come home from school when Mommy sat me down and told me he'd died. Oh God! I couldn't stop blubbering. There was something about him…he shouldn't have died! He was indomitable, which is why I'm sure, people have latched onto the hope that he's frozen in a vault somewhere.

diane disney miller DAUGHTER

After his brother Herb died, Dad was scheduled to go to Vandenberg Air Force Base on the day of the funeral. I remember standing by the grave and I saw a plane overhead and I've always thought it was Dad.

It was not for lack of love that he didn't go to Herb's funeral. He never ever went to funerals. He went to one once and said, "I hope no one ever has to go through this for me." So we tried to make his funeral so people didn't have to go through it. We kept it very private.

ray bradbury AUTHOR

Richard Schickel was going to interview me about Walt. Then he called me and said, "Walt died this morning, do you still want to have lunch?"

I said, "That's all the more reason. I *want* to talk about him. It's a terrible day." My mother had died a month before Walt, and to me both deaths were devastating.

fulton burley
"GOLDEN HORSESHOE REVUE" STAR

It hurt me deeply when Walt passed away. My mind immediately flashed back to a time we were having lunch together: Walt had picked up a cigarette with a filter on it, broke the filter off, lit it and took a puff. He caught me watching him and said, "You're looking at me quizzically, Fulton."

"Ah, yes, Uncle Walt." (I called him Uncle Walt.)

"Well, I'll tell you," he said. "My daughter gave me these cigarettes. She gave me two cartons of them at Christmas. She said, 'Dad, the way you're coughing, please use these cigarettes instead.' I promised her I would, but as you've noticed, I didn't tell her *how* I would use them." To Walt, a promise was a promise.

bob gurr   IMAGINEER

I remember Roger Broggie walked in just before lunch and he was totally gray and said, "Walt's gone; go home," and walked out. As I went out the door, the other employees were all silent. No one spoke to each other. It was like…just go home. I remember the day was rather chilly and moist with very heavy smog. I lived in Orange County and that was the longest, most awful drive home. The world had stopped.

ollie johnston   ANIMATOR

I was at my desk when Clark Mallory came into my office and said, "It just came over the news—Walt Disney's dead."

God, all the air went out of me. I went to Frank Thomas and told him. We just kind of looked at each other and I said, "Let's go home." About a week later, I remember sitting next to my wife and I began crying. I put my head in her lap and just cried.

john hench   ARTIST

We had heard from the back-lot employees, who were connected very closely with the hospital, the bad news that Walt was seriously ill. Still, when I got the news that Walt had actually died—total collapse.

jack speirs WRITER

After Walt had died, I went out one evening to get my car. And along came Walt's brother Roy. He was walking slow. He stepped out on the curb and stopped. He just stood there and took a long look around the Studio. He slowly looked the whole place over. Together, he and Walt had built all of this—and now Walt was gone—just gone. Roy dropped his head, looked at the ground, walked across the lot, got in his car and drove away. It was one of the saddest things I have ever seen.

roy e. disney NEPHEW

Just after Walt's operation, when he had come back to the Studio, they were finishing up *The Happiest Millionaire*. Bill Anderson said Walt watched a rough cut and just teared up and cried through it.

After Walt died, Bill said, "What am I going to do with this movie?" The thing really needed some work with the scissors. He said, "I know we ought to cut this, but Walt loved it!"

What a dilemma. First of all, Walt was sicker than hell when he saw the film. He was very emotional and who knows if he was emotional about his own situation or responding to the movie? Still, Bill couldn't bring himself to touch it and the film was released probably forty minutes longer than it should have been.

kurt russell ACTOR

When I was over at Universal working on a western while under contract at Disney, I was shooting a close-up and noticed there was some hubbub going on off camera. Then everybody went quiet. They were looking at me and I thought "What the hell's this?"

This guy came over to me and said, "I'm sorry to tell you this, Kurt, but Walt Disney died." They were all very sweet. The director asked me if I was okay to work and I said, "Oh yeah, sure. Go ahead."

His death was a surprise and I was saddened by it. But, I don't look at death as some sort of finality. It's sad you won't be able to spend time with somebody, but it makes you appreciate the time you had together. At that moment, I immediately appreciated the time I shared with Walt more than ever.

dick nunis THEME PARK EXECUTIVE

I was driving to work when I heard on the radio that Walt had died. I picked up the phone and called my boss, Card Walker, and asked, "Should we *not* open the Park?"

He said, "I don't know, let me get back to you." He called back in just a few minutes and said, "Open it."

"God, Card!" I said. "I think our people are going to be really upset."

He responded, "Lilly made this decision and I'll tell you what she said, 'Walt would say the show *must* go on.'" I got tears in my eyes.

So we opened and got blasted by the press. But you know what Van France and I did that day? I called him up to my office and said, "Van, we've got to start worrying about the next training book." That's when we came up with the idea of *The Traditions* concept so that Walt's words, traditions and philosophies would go on forever. We had a rough format by the end of the day. So the day Walt died, the show did go on.

ℒASTING IMPRESSIONS

kevin corcoran ACTOR

Everyone talks about "Where were you when John Kennedy was killed?" To me, Walt's death was much more devastating. He had an important impact on my life and still does. Every place I work, people say to me, "Oh, you were trained by Walt! Come and help us." I learned, basically, everything I know about filmmaking from Walt and his handpicked Studio professionals.

dick nunis THEME PARK EXECUTIVE

The most valuable thing I learned from Walt was the importance of people. I've learned that the higher you go in an organization, the less you do, the more you worry, and the more you depend on people. I think Walt depended on people a great deal, probably more than they realize. He had the intuitive ability to be as nice to a person busing the tables as to the president of a company and everybody in between.

mary costa VOICE OF SLEEPING BEAUTY

When I was a little girl, my father, who had died when I was very young, gave me a kaleidoscope and I would look at it for an hour at a time. Ironically, Walt once asked me, "Do you like kaleidoscopes?" (It really shocked me.) He said, "That's the way I want you to think. I want those colors to change all the time inside of your mind and translate into your speaking voice. You can tell most anything about a person by the way they speak or the way they sound. You can hear all those different kaleidoscopic colors. I want you to think about that." Little did Walt know, I would think about that throughout my life.

sharon baird MOUSEKETEER

Walt Disney wanted the Mouseketeers to call him Uncle Walt. We respected him so much though, we couldn't call him Uncle Walt. We called him Mr. Disney. But if he were here today, I would call him Uncle, *Uncle* Walt to make up for all the years I didn't call him "Uncle Walt." Now that I'm older, I understand what it would have meant to him to have us call him Uncle Walt.

richard sherman SONGWRITER

Walt had a great love for the song "Feed the Birds." The image came out of the book *Mary Poppins;* we used it as a symbol of kindness. Many times, late on Fridays, he'd call us into his office and say, "What have you been working on?" We'd chat for a while and then he'd say, "Dick, play that song for me." As I played and sang "Feed the Birds," he'd gaze out the window, get misty-eyed and say, "That's what it's all about, isn't it?"

After Walt died, the piano was still in his office for another year and sometimes my brother and I would go in on Friday afternoons to play for him. We felt his presence.

kurt russell ACTOR

Years after Mr. Disney died, I was still at the Studio making movies and there was a common cry, "Nothing's changed." Everybody was trying to hold on to what Walt would have done or what Walt would have liked.

I was older then, about twenty four-years old, and felt that my time was probably coming to an end at the Studio because my interests had changed. We were discussing a project and somebody said for the one hundredth time, "The thing about this is things haven't changed. Walt would have…"

I said, "You know, that's the problem with you guys. Things *would have* changed if Walt were alive. Things would be *very* different. They would *not* be the same. Walt always wanted to change things. That's exactly what I don't understand, right now, is that you're trying to hold on to what you think is a mindset. Walt would never allow his mind to remain the same."

They looked at me funny and I couldn't explain myself because that's what Walt represented to me. He was someone who was constantly aware of what might be fun to do, not necessarily cutting edge or different or what would blow people away, but what might be fun. I remember he would always say, "Wouldn't that be fun?"

harrison "buzz" price
RESEARCH CONSULTANT

I've always regretted my inability to grasp that I was in the epicenter of a historical occurrence. I had lunch with the man every week for the last eight years of his life; we would sit together and talk about his latest enthusiasms— How do we approach this? How do we measure that? What can we do to understand it? I took Walt for granted.

dean jones ACTOR

I think what impressed me most was his genius for being himself. He imprinted his character on the entire output of a movie studio and extended his feelings and points of view into American culture through his amusement parks.

lucille carroll ryman
SISTER OF DISNEY ARTIST

After Walt died, my brother Herb Ryman's appendix burst and he was in a coma for almost two days. The only thing he remembered during that time was a dream he had.

He was ascending stairs and surrounded by bright colored lights. He thought, "Ah, isn't this wonderful! This must be heaven." He got to the top of the stairs and on a high stool sat Walt, who ordered, "Herbie, you get back there! Go back! Go back! We don't want you here." Herbie was so hurt; he felt they didn't want him in heaven.

When he woke up, he was almost crying because the dream was so real to him. That afternoon, George Davis came to the hospital to see him and said, "Herb, how soon can you get out of here? I've been assigned to work on Tokyo Disneyland and I won't do it unless you're on the project, too."

Herbie told George about the dream and George said, "That's what Walt was trying to tell you, Herb, you *have* to work on Tokyo Disneyland!" Herbie agreed. He thought Walt was saying, "Heaven can wait; there's work for you to do."

ruth warrick ACTRESS

During my career, I have worked with two greats: Walt Disney (on *Song of the South*) and Orson Welles (on *Citizen Kane*). The one thing, I would say, they had most in common was their boyish delight in their work. Orson once said, "As you go, you find that work is not a four-letter word. It's the thing you can get the most joy out of. The whole thing is that you just have to choose the most important thing in your life. You must follow your heart's desire. Don't worry about the money, just *do* it because that's what God created you to do and be."

People say, "Orson said that?" I say, "yes," although Walt could have said it too.

hayley mills ACTRESS

A lot of Walt's personal philosophy has rubbed off on me. He was absolutely right, you *have* to focus on the good things. I think he really did love people. Only the cynics say, "He was onto a good thing and saw he could make a lot of money." Walt believed in what he was doing. He believed in being a positive force for good. He believed in people and that was why he was successful.

bobby burgess MOUSEKETEER

When Walt was alive, I used to walk down Main Street at Disneyland and glance up at his apartment over the Fire Station, hoping to see his face peeking out of the window. I still do that, even today. His spirit lives on in that magical place.

john hench ARTIST

Disneyland is haunted all right. I feel his spirit, especially at one of the two entranceways. Walt understood the function of an entranceway, or threshold, as he called it. The threshold is supposed to embrace you. It's where you feel like you're entering some very special place. And how intuitive he was to create the surrounding berm to shut out the outside world.

ray bradbury AUTHOR

Watch him on the old *Disneyland* TV show. He was Walt Disney. You really *believed* in him. It came from within. There was a rumor that he had been frozen in a cryogenic mortuary to be revived in later years. Nonsense! I said. He's alive now. People at the Studio speak of him as if he were present! There's immortality for you. Who needs cryogenics!

paul carlson ANIMATOR

I remember somebody asked Walt what he wanted to be remembered for and he said, "I'm a storyteller. Of all the things I've ever done, I'd like to be remembered as a *storyteller*."

ACKNOWLEDGMENTS AND SOURCES

ACKNOWLEDGMENTS This book was a group project. It could never have been realized without the help and cooperation of so many people—more than can possibly be listed here. We honor our friends Ollie Johnston, Frank Thomas, Marc Davis, Ward Kimball, and Joe Grant, who's memories of Walt served as inspiration for this book.

We are deeply indebted to Diane Disney Miller, who supported this project from conception. Thanks, also, to Roy and Patty Disney for generously sharing their time and delightful recollections with us.

Richard and Katherine Greene are "our heros," for sharing quotes from family interviews they conducted for their book *The Man Behind the Magic: The Story of Walt Disney.* Were it not for the Greenes, some invaluable memories would be missing from this book. We are most grateful to Ray Bradbury for the exquisite introduction he penned, obviously inspired by his love and respect for Walt.

What book about Walt is complete without a bow to the Walt Disney Studio Archives—Dave Smith, Robert Tieman, Collette Espino, and Madame Becky Cline. We appreciate Jim Fanning and his skilled photo research, as well as archivist Ed Squair, who ferreted out such obscurities from the immense Disney Photo Library, as the family vacation snapshots found in Walt's desk at the time of his death featured in the "Goodbye So Soon" chapter. Additionally, we tip our hats to Hugh Chitwood of the Walt Disney Imagineering Slide Library for locating unforgettable images of Walt.

Heartfelt appreciation to those who helped connect us with celebrities, including veteran Disney publicist Arlene Ludwig and honorary Mouseketeer Lorraine Santoli, as well as Hollywood's "Gentleman Jim" of the publicity world Julian Myers, veteran publicist Bob Palmer, and legendary Disney flack Leonard Shannon. We give four stars to Hollywood's critically-acclaimed film critic Leonard Maltin and his awesome wife Alice for their support and friendship. To our agent, New York's famed Richard Curtis, we give humble thanks for his many professional courtesies.

It was a joy to work with Disney's publishing group, namely Ken Shue, who's genuine affection for Walt accentuated the fun of creating this labor of love. It was great working with his team, including Brent Ford, Susan Saroff, and Ed Jaciow. We give a special salute to Design Office in San Francisco for their fine efforts, as well as Janice Kawamoto, who helped launch the design process.

We kiss the ring of Charles Solomon—animation historian, journalist, author, bon vivant and friend. Like a delivering angel, he swooped in to help Amy edit *Remembering Walt,* while Howard concentrated on writing *The Tarzan Chronicles.* Also, thanks to our editor Wendy Lefkon for her guidance on this project.

We owe a special debt to Bob Penfield, Bob Broughton and Lorraine Davis, who introduced us to retired Disney employees, and are eternally grateful to Kat Cressida and Tracey Miller, who helped lift the transcription load.

Additional thanks go to Disney scholars Paul Anderson and J.B. Kaufman; film historians Karl Thiede, Scott MacQueen, and Marc Wannamaker. We also appreciate David Sokol at *Disney Magazine,* Andreas Deja, Dan and Elly Wolf, Zelda Wong, Betsy Baytos, Paula Sigman-Lowry, Bob Board, Willie Ito, Jack Taylor, Carl Bell, Elaine LaZelle, David Collier, Nathan Sternfeld, Melody Strite, Lynn Weatherford-Bedri, Audrey McIlwrath, Melody Schmidt, John and Janice Boothe, Ruth Green-Blumenthal, and Jim Lynn.

In closing, we give heartfelt thanks to Walt's niece, Dorothy Puder, and her husband, Rev. Glenn Puder. Through the kindness of our friend Mary Alice O'Connor, we had a delightful meeting with the couple. Then, at the close of our meeting, the Puders invited us to join hands as Dorothy offered a prayer and a blessing upon this book, those who helped create it, and those who will read its contents. Working on this book has been a blessing in itself; we feel privileged to have played a role in preserving the larger-than-life memory of a most remarkable man, Walt Disney.

SOURCES Many quotes from Walt's immediate family are courtesy of Richard & Katherine Greene, who conducted extensive interviews for their book *The Man Behind the Magic: The Story of Walt Disney* and generously granted us access to them. Additional anecdotes have been excerpted from existing interviews, located in the Walt Disney Studio Archives, conducted by Richard Hubler, Bob Thomas, Pete Martin, Don Peri, Dave Smith, Jay Horan, Steve Hulett, David Tietyen, Christopher Finch and Linda Rosenkrantz. Publications include, *Disney Magazine, E Ticket, The Mouse Club, Storyboard Magazine, The Comics Journal, Walt Disney's Railroad Story,* by Michael Broggie, and *Club 55,* a book dedicated to Disneyland's original employees, courtesy of Van Arsdale France.

PHOTO CAPTIONS